The Way Out

The Way Out

Christianity, Politics, and the Future of the African-American Community

TED WILLIAMS III

WIPF & STOCK · Eugene, Oregon

THE WAY OUT
Christianity, Politics, and the Future of the African American Community

Copyright © 2014 Ted Williams III. All rights reserved. Except for brief quotations in critical publications or reviews, no part of this book may be reproduced in any manner without prior written permission from the publisher. Write: Permissions, Wipf and Stock Publishers, 199 W. 8th Ave., Suite 3, Eugene, OR 97401.

Wipf & Stock
An Imprint of Wipf and Stock Publishers
199 W. 8th Ave., Suite 3
Eugene, OR 97401

www.wipfandstock.com

ISBN 13: 978-1-62032-473-8

Manufactured in the U.S.A.

To Roslyn, Gabrielle,
Amaris, and Theodore IV

You give me the strength
to fight for a better world.

*This is written in the hope that our
future can be much brighter.*

Contents

Acknowledgments ix

Preface xi

1. African Americans and Christianity: A Shared Narrative 1
2. New Wineskins: Rethinking European and African American Responsibilities 12
3. Rejecting a Depraved Culture 29
4. The African American Church: Reclaiming a Legacy 42
5. Political Engagement: Developing a New Agenda 52
6. Countering a Culture of Violence 64
7. Marriage and Family Policy: A Foundation for the Future 70
8. Education Reform: The Civil Rights Issue of This Generation 83
9. Entrepreneurship: The Key to Prosperity 92
10. Personal Reflections 99

Bibliography 103

Index 112

Acknowledgments

This book is dedicated primarily to my amazing wife. Thank you, Roslyn, for bearing with me and sharing the load during the arduous process of writing this book. You truly are the wind beneath my wings. I love you with all of my heart. Thank you also to the wonderful members of my family who laid the foundation for my life. Mom and Dad, you guys provided the launching pad for everything I currently am. I thank you for your love, sacrifices, and hard work. You have given me a tremendous model for my life and family.

Thank you to my grandparents who have gone on to glory, Theodore Sr., Eliza, and LC. Your example was the foundation for what we all have today. Thank you especially to my grandmother Shirley, who is still with us. You are the greatest example of love and family I have ever seen. We all wish for many more years with you!

Thank you also to my brother Brandon. Since the day you were born, you have made me strive to be a great example for you. Thanks for being my best friend all these years.

Thank you to all of my aunts, uncles, cousins and extended family. I treasure the times we spend together and appreciate you tremendously. Thank you for inspiring me, encouraging me, bearing with my growth in life, and showing me the kind of love that many don't have. You have shaped me in ways you cannot imagine.

Thank you to my new family, Renee, Ronald, Ronnie, and all of our cousins, aunts, etc. Thanks for extending your love and support to my family. I greatly appreciate you.

To my amazing church family at The Way Christian Ministries. The work that we do is the most important in the world. I

Acknowledgments

thank God for your support, love, and faithfulness. Let's continue to change the world for him!

To my TORN the Musical and 3rd Dimension artistic family with whom I have produced and performed for years. Your talent amazes me. Thanks for allowing me to share the stage with you!

To my colleagues at WYCC and the City Colleges of Chicago. You keep me on my toes and continue to challenge me intellectually. It is an honor to serve with you.

To all of my fellow political activists in Chicago and around the nation. You inspire me to continue to fight for justice in our world.

To the wonderful scholars at Kennedy-King College, Chicago State University, Upward Bound, New Life Celebration Christian Academy, the Dance Gallery, and the host of artistic programs in which I have worked. Your energy, passion, and zeal for learning have inspired me in ways you cannot imagine. You are the fuel for this work and the reason I am optimistic about our future. Continue to believe that our world can be different and it will. I hope this book will inspire and direct you to move forward as agents of change in your lives and careers. Thank you for motivating me.

To the three children my wife and God have blessed me to have, Gabrielle, Amaris, and Theodore IV. You are the reason for my hope in the future. Remember that the greatest accomplishment that you can have in your life is to know that you made a difference for someone else. Daddy loves you guys!

And lastly, I thank God, without whom none of this would be possible.

Preface

In 1619 twenty African slaves arrived in Jamestown, Virginia, aboard a Dutch ship. They were brought to America as human chattel to fuel a burgeoning economy that eventually would become the greatest in the world. For these men and women, the years that followed would be nothing short of incredible in terms of both the pain and the progress that would be experienced. The story of the African American is one replete with the anguish of discrimination and slavery coupled with the power of faith. This is evidenced by a devotion to God that empowered them to triumph over the evil institution of slavery and to win a variety of major social victories over the course of just a few hundred years.

Yet this story is not simple by any means. After arriving in a culture that valued them solely for the labor they provided, this group would experience some of the worst physical and mental oppression known to man. Laws would establish a system of slavery, oppression, Jim Crow segregation, and discrimination that would isolate this group from the American mainstream for centuries. At the heart of much of this inhumane treatment was the Christian faith that the Puritans and Pilgrims brought from Europe. So while American leaders extolled the virtues of Christianity and its implications for this new nation, these same leaders used that religion to systematically oppress and exterminate millions of people. How? Their understanding of humankind's equality as found in the biblical scriptures along with the writings of men like Thomas Jefferson could not possibly have included groups like the Africans or Native Americans. America created and bought into a story of racial identity that made it impossible for these people to be considered fully equal human beings. Furthermore, Americans found great justification for these positions in their beloved Bible as they read the stories of Ham, and scriptures that directed Christians to be patient and loving in the face of slavery and oppression. Christianity seemed like the perfect religion to support this bifurcated class system. As they passed this religion on to their African slaves, these slaves embraced its message willingly. Rather than desire social justice as fully equal human beings, the slaves were encouraged to wait on heaven for their salvation. Consequently, the system continued, relatively unchallenged, for the next two hundred years.

So the obvious question is: Should the oppressed group have rejected the religion of their oppressor? And more importantly, should twenty-first-century African Americans do the same?

My conclusion may surprise most. After all of the destruction on this community in the name of Christianity and racial superiority, the Christian faith still represents the greatest hope for the elevation of both the African American people and this nation as a whole.

It was through the horrors of slavery that African people connected with the God of Abraham, Moses, and Jesus. Currently, African Americans embrace Christianity at higher levels than any group in this nation. The civil rights movement, the faith that allowed the slaves to survive, and the current prevalence of religion in the African American community are all examples of Christianity's lasting social impact.

Yet the African American community today represents a paradox of sorts. As an African American, a Christian, and a political commentator, this challenge has been a source of great concern for most of my life. While we retain a great spiritual tradition and culture, our collective lifestyles, leadership, and political focus fails to reflect this tradition. Consequently we find ourselves, like the rest of America, facing a severe spiritual crisis. While close to 40 percent of children in the United States are raised without a father, for African Americans this number has reached catastrophic proportions at just under 70 percent.[1] Furthermore, while American

---

1. Population Reference Bureau, analysis of data from the U.S. Census Bureau, Census 2000 Supplementary Survey, 2001 Supplementary Survey,

Preface

divorce rates, abortion rates, and incarceration rates are the highest in the world, African Americans hold the unenviable distinction of leading the nation in all of these categories. Yet we still find our churches filled every week by people praying and searching for direction. And while many take this fact to be an indictment against Christianity, I look at it as a great opportunity for moral and social elevation. The moral crisis facing this nation is grave. Unfortunately this crisis has had a more significant impact on the African American community than most. America must embrace a comprehensive plan for transformation that is biblical, political, and sociological, and offers solutions that put responsibility equally on the individual, the faith community, and civil society. These solutions must be individual and collective, requiring both institutional involvement and personal responsibility. Yet at the core there must be an understanding of the moral and spiritual direction found, historically, in the church and faith tradition. This reclamation of a transformative faith and an understanding of the answers it provides is the greatest need of the hour.

The more I watch our nation's political leaders attempt to solve our greatest crises, the more convinced I am of the social relevance of biblical tenets. Along with the spiritual elevation that is possible only through the church experience, African American leadership must recognize its political opportunities as well. Both the Democrat and Republican parties must be held accountable for responding to the core needs of this diverse community. It is time for a new agenda, one that re-evaluates old methods of problem solving and reinstitutes the role of faith at the center of an overall social agenda. Future generations require this focus.

There is a billboard in my grandmother's neighborhood on the South Side of Chicago that I have seen my entire life. Every time I drive to her home, I am reminded of God's call for both myself and my community. The billboard simply says, "Righteousness exalteth a nation: but sin is a reproach to any people" (Prov 14:34, KJV).

Truly, if America is going to survive as a nation, it must be through a commitment to moral principles and public policies that

---

2002–2011 American Community Survey.

reflect God's purposes. This is especially true of African Americans. An innovative, faith-based, and holistic approach to political and social engagement is critical for our future. It is for this reason that I write this work to all Americans as a path of light to transform suffering communities.

1

African Americans and Christianity

A Shared Narrative

> *I love the pure, peaceable, and impartial Christianity of Christ: I therefore hate the corrupt, slaveholding, women-whipping, cradle-plundering, partial and hypocritical Christianity of the land.*
>
> —Fredrick Douglass[1]

African Americans have a rich history with the Christian faith. From Christianity's historic connection to the African continent to the arrival of the first slave in 1619, the abolition of slavery, and the Civil Rights Movement, Christianity has been an integral part of this narrative. It has touched every aspect of the African American experience including education, politics, economics, family life, and even healthcare. Individually, the Christian faith provided strength through the horrors of slavery, and the fuel for the rich artistic culture that grew out of these experiences.

1. Douglass, "Slaveholding Religion and the Religion of Christ."

The Way Out

Collectively, the church served as the most significant social institution and a holistic connecting point to the collective needs of the community for hundreds of years. Even today, we see both of these traditions continue in the artistic, social, academic, and political life of America's forty million citizens of African descent. African Americans are the most consistently faithful ethnic group to the Christian faith and its imprint has left an indelible mark on most aspects of the culture. Arguably, there may be no more universally consistent influence on this community than Christianity. Consequently, any conversation about the challenges and opportunities facing African Americans must begin by exploring the implications of this faith. In examining the future, we should begin by exploring the past. Consequently, following are some highlights of the relationship between African Americans and Christianity in the United States.

1780   The Methodist denomination requires all its itinerate preachers to set their slaves free. This act precedes the Emancipation Proclamation by over eighty years.

1784   The first General Conference (the Christmas Conference) of the newly formed Methodist Episcopal Church forbids its members to own slaves. In this same year, Richard Allen, widely considered to be the "father of the black church," is ordained a Methodist minister. He would go on to found the African Methodist Episcopal Church.

1831   Nat Turner leads an insurrection in Southampton Virginia. At least fifty-seven whites are killed before the revolt is put down. Turner, a Christian minister, believed that God called him to pursue freedom.

1843   Black Presbyterian pastor Henry Highland Garnet gives a fiery "Address to the Slaves," in which he calls for slaves to rebel.

African Americans and Christianity

1843 Isabella Baumfree (1797–1883) changes her name to Sojourner Truth and begins a career as preacher, abolitionist, and feminist.

1854 The Presbyterian Church establishes Ashmun Institute (later renamed Lincoln University) in Pennsylvania to train black men for missions and ministry.

1856 The Methodist Episcopal Church North establishes Ohio's Wilberforce University, named for the famous British abolitionist, to educate blacks. The AME Church, under the leadership of Bishop Daniel A. Payne, purchased Wilberforce University in 1863, making it the first college for African Americans owned and operated by a black organization.[2]

1906 African American Preacher William Seymour begins the Azusa Street Revival. This nine-year revival is considered to be the genesis of the modern Pentecostal movement, a national catalyst for interracial worship, and is called one of the hundred most influential events of the millennium by *Life* magazine.

1945 Adam Clayton Power Jr., a Baptist minister, is elected to the House of Representatives. He is the first African American congressman from New York, and one of only two in the nation at the time. Powell's work in the faith community was the driving force behind his ascension to national office and his role as one of the greatest national and international civil rights leaders of his era.

1955 The Montgomery Bus Boycott begins the modern Civil Rights Movement. Its most visible leader is a young preacher from Atlanta named Dr. Martin Luther King Jr. He saw the work of liberating oppressed people as the work of God and drew his greatest inspiration and direction from the words of Christ.

---

2. Miller, "Black Christianity."

The Way Out

1970 Dr. James Cone publishes the landmark work *A Black Theology of Liberation*, paving a new connection between Christianity and the struggle of the African American community known as liberation theology. His work influenced countless educators, ministers, and political figures to retain a commitment to biblical faith while pursuing social equality. His most famous quote is, "For me, the burning theological question was, how can I reconcile Christianity and Black Power, Martin Luther King Jr.'s idea of nonviolence, and Malcolm X's 'by any means necessary' philosophy?"[3]

2008 Barack Obama is elected to the nation's highest office. The African American church is, arguably, the most dependable and organized constituent group in his campaign. Many contend that without the fierce loyalty of the African American church his election would have been impossible.

Consider the additional examples of Christianity's use as a tool for the liberation of people of African descent. The end of slavery was precipitated by the British abolitionist and legislator Wilber Wilberforce. His firm and unwavering Christian witness was the vital force that helped to turn the tide of the British legislature toward the end of slavery in the nation. Contrary to the modern idea of secular progressive social thought, it was Christianity that pushed the agenda of equality during the time of Wilberforce. Hiram Revels, the first African American U.S. Senator, is another of example of this history. Revels was an ordained African Methodist Episcopal minister, a chaplain of a Negro regiment during the Civil War, and an minister/organizer of churches in Mississippi, Maryland, Kansas, Illinois, Tennessee, and Kentucky. Both his oratory and writing skills were honed in the church, making him a powerful and articulate defender of both African American progress and the Christian faith.

Benjamin Elijah Mays was one of the most important educators of African Americans in U.S. history. Mays, a Baptist minister, served as the president of Morehouse College, the first president of

---

3. Cone, *Black Theology and Black Power*, viii.

African descent of the Atlanta school board, an early mentor to Dr. Martin Luther King Jr., and an intellectual shaper of the modern Civil Rights Movement. Mays was the dean of Howard University's School of Religion and used his theological grounding to vociferously rebut segregation and racism in America. Lastly, the most famous civil rights leader in American history, Dr. Martin Luther King Jr., had an intimate relationship with Christianity and drew his greatest inspiration from the faith. Dr. King's contributions to American justice and equality cannot be divorced from the religion that influenced them. Raised in the African American church and academically trained in a seminary, Dr. King's most significant influence as an international leader came from his faith. The argument can clearly be made that without Christ there would have been no Martin Luther King Jr.

It is obvious that one cannot tell about the history of African Americans without telling a history of Christianity. For those who deny the positive role of Christianity in the struggle of Americans of African descent, they ignore an overwhelming quantity of historic data. However, there is no simple narrative to describe the entirety of this complex relationship. There exists a complicated and often controversial reality when taking into account all aspects of this association. As Fredrick Douglass articulated, he often vacillated between loving the most praiseworthy aspects of Christianity while understanding how the faith was used to subjugate millions of African Americans. Like many, he wrestled to reconcile this fact. What Douglass found, in addition to millions of others, was that it is quite possible to reject the racism of the slave master, while seeing Christianity as the hope of the future. Understanding this connection is crucial to any conversations on future progress.

American slavery and the subsequent years of discrimination perpetrated against African people were nefarious injustices for which America has yet to fully atone. It is no secret that in a nation of substantial wealth and opportunity, many of those who are currently disenfranchised are people of color. The wealth of the average European American family is twenty times greater than that of the average African American family.[4] Additionally, African American

---

4. Kochhar et al., "Wealth Gaps Rise."

communities are faced with higher crime rates, failing schools, and an unemployment rate that consistently tops the national average. It is clear that the hundreds of years of governmental policies designed to disaffect this group of people have worked to achieve this goal. In this way, the United States was not founded on the principles of equality and still has a long road ahead to secure this dream for its African citizens. Yet in this picture of despair, we can still find a silver lining.

Christianity, though used as a racist tool of the slave master, became a source of aspiration, a tool for education, and a path for liberation for many slaves. This occurred in spite of a living in a nation that saw people of African descent as less than equal not only in the eyes of man, but also in the eyes of God. And while many look at the obvious use of Christianity in pushing the slaveholders' agenda, most miss both the liberation and inspiration that came from that same religion. It is understandably difficult to comprehend the two corresponding realities.

Consequently, it is appropriate to begin our analysis of the current condition of this community by examining a story of biblical parallel. The biblical story of Joseph is the story of a man whose destiny was forever altered by his brothers selling him into slavery. Joseph, who was sold at the age of seventeen, suffered for years because of his family's betrayal. The most significant years of his life were spent at the hands of a brutal Egyptian regime. Years of lost potential, physical struggle, and oppression resulted from the unjust and wicked treatment he received from his brothers.

Years later Joseph ultimately understood that this experience produced a greater outcome. For this reason, his energy was focused on recognizing the opportunities of the present rather than on the injustices of the past. Years after his suffering ended, Joseph's response to his treatment was to tell his brothers, "You intended to harm me, but God intended it for good to accomplish what is now being done, the saving of many lives" (Gen 50:20 NIV). Joseph's position of slavery eventually allowed him access to the greatest power center on earth at the time. His humility led him to ascend to a place in which he became the second most significant leader in Egypt, next to Pharaoh. Ultimately, this provided him the authority to distribute life-saving resources during a period of famine in Egypt. The great irony of the story is that the same people who sold him into slavery found themselves depending on him for sustenance during their time of crisis. Rather than using this position for vengeance or self-gratification, Joseph understood his unique calling and the opportunity his position afforded him to help the masses.

There may not be a greater parallel to the collective plight of Americans of African descent.

God used Joseph's slavery to save thousands of lives and elevate him to a status that he would have never achieved otherwise. He was placed in a position of influence and opportunity that he eventually used to benefit an entire nation. Like Joseph, the reprehensible actions perpetrated against African Americans were ultimately used to secure a greater purpose. Years ago I attended a conference hosted by the organization World Vision. At the conference a woman from Zambia spoke, describing the great destitution faced by her family, community, and nation. Her story was powerful as she described great poverty, AIDS, and civil unrest. Yet what she said about the solution will stick with me for the rest of my life. She said that she looked to the African American community as a crucial part of her nation's ultimate deliverance. I remember wondering why she chose to mention this. Her rationale was that through slavery, African Americans were now in a unique position in the United States to impact the entire world. Additionally, she saw African Americans as uniquely qualified to lead in this fight because of their natural connection to the continent coupled with the size of their collective economy. In her mind, slavery, while evil, had produced a people with a heart to understand the plight of the oppressed, and the economic and political power to effect change for billions of others. Her assessment was both humbling and inspiring. For the first time I recognized the awesome responsibility for global leadership and economic development possessed by African Americans.

African Americans, compared to European Americans, are woefully behind. However, compared to most of the world, they are in a powerful economic position. The media rating company Nielson, along with the National Newspaper Publishers Association, released a report in 2011 that projected African American consumer buying power to reach $1.5 trillion by 2015.

The study, which focused on African American spending, media habits, and consumer trends, reported an increase in the number attending college or earning a degree to 44 percent for men and 53 percent for women.[5] Additionally, it showed that this combined buying power gives the African American community the sixteenth largest international Gross Domestic Product. This places them among the wealthiest and most educated population in the entire world. While this information fails to excuse the obvious disparities that exist in the American context, it provides a picture of a group with tremendous economic and social potential. It must be harnessed.

The United States still represents the greatest hope of economic, academic, and political opportunity for billions in the world. Ignoring this fact would be foolish. A truly accurate assessment of this picture reflects the concomitant realities of rampant injustice and tremendous freedom of opportunity. Our current political conversation fails to allow for a discussion grounded in the complexities of this symbiotic relationship. How can a nation so steeped in a history of discrimination for African people still offer the best chance of prosperity for this same group globally? Without a deep analysis of history that also takes into account current possibilities, this seems implausible. Yet the answer to this question is simple if viewed through the lens of possibility. The current economic and social condition of African Americans has placed them in a unique position to both empathize with the plight of those on the African continent and channel significant economic resources towards their development.

The 2000 African Growth and Opportunity Act (AGOA) is an example of this kind of unique opportunity. Signed into law and promoted heavily by members of the Congressional Black Caucus, this act moved the relationship between the United States and the African continent to one of trade and not simply financial assistance. The AGOA set up a system of reduced barriers to trade for a select

---

5. "State of the African-American Consumer."

number of African nations and allowed U.S. companies to more easily set up shop on the continent. A number of members of the Congressional Black Caucus were instrumental in promoting the original passage of this legislation and they continue to be ardent supporters. While this legislation may be imperfect, as it further encouraged U.S. companies to ship jobs offshore, it did represent a significant sea change in U.S. policy towards Africa. The AGOA and national efforts like it are the beginning of a new relationship with Africa, one that promotes mutually beneficial business partnerships and moves away from charity. It is the African American voice that has the potential to serve as the lynchpin for further U.S./Africa partnerships. Like Joseph, America's former slaves can provide this important leadership. His perceived misfortune ultimately became his greatest asset. In the same way, the African American community possesses a similar opportunity for global influence.

And while Christianity's role in the history of African Americans has been vital, its future role may be even more important. Christianity has come under attack in American culture in recent years. While America has one of the most church-going populations in the world, the connected ideologies of postmodernism and secularism have gained root in American culture. Examples of this trend include attacks against the use of the term Christmas, the censorship of public expressions of faith, and a popular culture that increasingly sees Christian moral values as antiquated and hostile towards American notions of freedom. While there are many other examples abound, they convey a larger hostility towards the tenets of the Christian faith in mainstream American culture.

In the African American community this trend has the potential to have an especially pernicious and damaging impact. Most urban communities represent a mixture of poverty, crime, and violence. Ironically, these areas also include an abundance of churches. Often critics of Christianity make the argument that this dynamic represents a failure of the church. Yet in these areas, churches are involved in food distribution, mentoring, employment, and act as a conduit between government programs and the populations that need them the most. Critics also argue that the separation of church and state precludes many of these churches from partnering with the government in their efforts to provide social services. Yet they often ignore the fact that there is no other institution that has the reach and the history of the church. Without the holistic work of communities of faith, the problems in urban America would be drastically worse.

Consider the unique story of the ministry in which I currently serve. In my work as a community college professor in the inner city of Chicago, I encounter men and women whose lives have been devastated by crime, a lack of economic opportunity, single-parent homes, poor education, and a culture of moral depravity. They have chosen to attend college for the possibility of social mobility, however, they are often hampered significantly by the conditions from which they've come. They are looking for success and their educational pursuits represent the beginning of this important quest. Yet what is often misunderstood is that secular education by itself often fails to provide the level of success for which these students strive. Why is this? As Dr. King said, "Intelligence plus character—that is the goal of true education." The missing piece is what the church can bring. Christianity has the ability to provide these students with the character development that is as crucial to their success as academic credentials. This is why, inevitably, my mentoring of these young men and women often includes the introduction of my personal faith and a connection to my ministry community. As many students have chosen a life of commitment to biblical principles, I have witnessed their transformation both academically and spiritually. Additionally, as they have given their lives in service to the church, they have overcome the societal ills common to their peers. Inner-city and fatherless African American males, who are especially prone to suffer from the aforementioned challenges, make up the majority of my current church ministry. As a result, I understand the great power of the church. Its ability to revolutionize the social and moral conditions under which so many are suffering cannot be overstated.

Given this reality, it is clear that one of the most destructive trends in our current culture is the movement away from faith. A study by the Lewis Center for Church Leadership at the Wesley Theological Seminary in Washington, DC, suggests that American church attendance is down for most denominations. According to the study, between 2001 and 2008 church attendance for all denominations fell on average by just under 15 percent.[6]

Church attendance in the United States has not kept up with population growth.[7] And while African Americans still report the highest level of church attendance (53 percent) and daily prayer (76 percent), these attendance declines have held steady in all ethnic groups. Increasingly, African Americans are among the unchurched in ways foreign to our experience in the United States. What will this change mean for communities of color in the future? This remains to be seen, however, we know that America's embrace of postmodern and culturally relative approaches to morality have had a deleterious impact on all communities, especially those of color.

Faith has served to provide moral and social protection for all groups historically. For this reason, I am convinced that the greatest hope for African Americans is the revitalization of faith at the core of community building. The social shift away from the central role of faith has potential ramifications beyond what most have comprehended. Realizing this, we must reject efforts to negate and diminish faith at the core of the solutions necessary to uplift communities of color. We face an overwhelming set of challenges that require a variety of approaches. Yet recognizing and reinforcing the historic and critical role of the Christian faith among African Americans is imperative for anyone serious about implementing long-term holistic solutions to the current difficulties.

---

6. Weems, "No Shows."
7. Barnes and Lowry, "Special Report."

2

New Wineskins

Rethinking European and African American Responsibilities

> *Our Negro problem, therefore, is not of the Negro's making. No group in our population is less responsible for its existence. But every group is responsible for its continuance. . . . Both races need to understand that their rights and duties are mutual and equal and their interests in the common good are identical. . . . There is no help or healing in appraising past responsibilities or in present apportioning of praise or blame. The past is of value only as it aids in understanding the present; and an understanding of the facts of the problem—a magnanimous understanding by both races—is the first step toward its solution.*
>
> —Isabel Wilkerson[1]

Both European and African Americans must embrace new ways of thinking and new behaviors when confronted with the race issue. This is vital to the progress of our nation in addressing an area that has plagued us for so long. Both groups must not only understand the progress this nation has made, but must also

---

1. Wilkerson, *Warmth of Other Suns*, 543.

New Wineskins

wrestle with questions of continued injustice, reparations, and a mentality of victimization that continues to cripple millions. As with many issues, the Christian faith can play a substantial role in developing remedies for these conundrums. However, reaching this remedy will take a shift in thinking on the part of both groups that rejects conversations rooted in self-interest, and embraces biblically consistent and politically astute ways of thinking and acting with respect to this issue.

The election of Barack Obama to the nation's highest office represents a great triumph, on one hand. It represents America moving beyond the racial demons of its past. It showed the world that the promise of the United States is real and true. It truly reflects a level of progress that many thought they would never live to see. However, in this victory, we have still missed something important. Many believed that Obama's election would represent a brighter day, a post-racial America. In fact, in many ways, it has served to bring our nation's darkest demons to the surface. The level of vitriol and acrimony faced by the President has been tremendous. He has faced extreme obstructionism from members of Congress and a number of personal attacks surrounding his ethnicity and Americanism.

Yet, this does not represent the most egregious missed opportunity of America in his election. Contrary to popular belief, the election of Barack Obama should not be a victory solely for African Americans. While some African Americans treat him as the savior of the race, and certain segments of the European American population are afraid of him, the reality is that he is as European as he is African. His mother is from Kansas and his father is from Kenya. Unfortunately, for most this makes him strictly a "black man," however his ethnic identity is more complicated and speaks to a greater American historic conversation about race. America's greatest missed opportunity is redefining its long-held definitions about race and ethnicity.

In 1924, the state of Virginia enacted the Racial Integrity Act, a series of laws defining race for the purposes of achieving and preserving racial segregation. In this act, the state called for all citizens to be classified by race and mandated that anyone with at least one eighth African ancestry be considered a Negro. This law was known as the "one-drop rule," stating that persons of any ancestry mixed with Negro would automatically be classified as Negro.[2] Based on segregationist and eugenicist principles, this law made it a felony to misclassify a person's race. It was designed to protect the standard of whiteness and introduced the "hypo-descent" rule that assigned racially mixed persons with the status of the subordinate group.

Unfortunately, this inaccurate system of racial classification is alive and well in the United States today. It is the only reason that a person born of a European American mother and an African father would be considered "black." It makes little sense and separates the United States from the rest of the world on this issue. For Americans of all perspectives to move forward on race, we must recognize the unique opportunity with which Barack Obama presents this nation. As a biracial man, he represents a large swath of the American population. His success should do more to unite rather than divide us. Yet if we fail to recognize this chance to redefine our antiquated and racist system of classification, we will be no better off than before his election. It is time for us to expand our understanding and view of this critical issue.

We are all equally responsible for a redefinition of race in America. And while many progressives see faith as an impediment to progress in the area of racial unity, in fact, the truth is quite the opposite. Christianity can prove to be an effective asset in the battle for redefining our national approach to the conversation on race. Primarily, Christianity assumes a common identity for all of humankind that sees us in relationship to a perfect and loving God. The equality of all people is obvious when we consider not only God's perfect standard for humankind, but also his immense love for us all. In truth, what person can claim that they are better than another when viewed in this light? I would argue that Christianity is the greatest equalizer of humanity as our natural physical state is full of inequality. Yet in God's eyes, we are all the same. While Christianity has faced its own historic set of challenges around ethnic and class divisions, the core tenets of the faith promote racial

---

2. Davis, *Who Is Black?*

equality. The Christian standard is one of humility, patience, and selflessness, qualities often lacking in American conversations on race. Furthermore, the myriad examples of ethnic and class diversity found in Christian churches around the world is evidence of its equalizing power. During the struggle for racial equality in both the United States and South Africa in the past century, it was the church's example of multiethnic brotherhood that made a significant difference. Faith-based leaders such as Bishop Desmond Tutu and Dr. Martin Luther King Jr. used the Christian faith and the church's example to light a path for humility, love, and justice. Rather than looking at past challenges, we must recognize the great opportunity that exists for leadership on this issue within the Christian community. Through scripture this group possesses the theological blueprint for equality. When we fully understand the severe depravity of all, we understand our universal need for redemption. Whether the issue is race or a host of other challenges that plague our nation, a humble, pluralistic, and holistic Christianity still represents the greatest hope for the collective racial peace and prosperity that our nation desperately desires.

Unfortunately, our polarized political system limits our discussions of race strictly to conversations about who is to blame for the nation's challenges. However, with respect to the quagmire faced by African Americans, the story is much more complex. In light of a history of systemic oppression and discrimination, African Americans have proven relatively resilient. To have reached significant levels of individual achievement, given the horrible discrimination faced just fifty years ago, speaks volumes about what is possible. Senator Daniel Patrick Moynihan wrote in his famous 1965 US Labor Department Report, "That the Negro American has survived at all is extraordinary—a lesser people might simply have died out, as indeed others have. That the Negro community has not only survived, but in this political generation has entered national affairs as a moderate, humane, and constructive national force is the highest testament to the healing powers of the democratic ideal and the creative vitality of the Negro people."[3]

---

3. US Department of Labor, *Negro Family* (Moynihan Report), ch. 4.

The Way Out

I refuse to allow the government, our leaders, sociologists, or anyone else to sell me on the idea of an unavoidably bleak future. More importantly, I refuse to pass that viewpoint on to my students, mentees in the church, or my children. In 2002, when I began teaching in at Kennedy-King Community College in Chicago's Englewood neighborhood, my students vehemently rejected the possibility of America electing a president of African descent. In six short years their doubts were proven erroneous. It has yet to be fully measured the psychological damage enacted when a group of people is constantly told that they are incapable of success because of some invisible force or historic disadvantage. Why would any young person desire to work hard, given this perspective? The vast majority of these young people are going to struggle for motivation when they are constantly reminded that their chances for achievement are bleak. In response to these sentiments, many African American political groups have embraced a message of self-determination and community based solutions as the key to social mobility. Mainstream leadership would do well to embrace this agenda as well.

I do realize that the struggle has been difficult. I also realize that the effects of slavery will not disappear overnight. Senator Moynihan also states, "But it may not be supposed that the Negro American community has not paid a fearful price for the incredible mistreatment to which it has been subjected over the past three centuries."[4] Slavery and discrimination have had great consequences. Paul Robeson, the international singer and activist, said, "I refuse to let my personal success, as a part of a fraction of 1 percent of the Negro people, explain away the injustices of 14 million of my people."[5] The problems faced by African Americans have a large institutional and systematic history. Any notions that they are the result of the amalgamation of individual failures are erroneous. The phenomenon of economic despair repeated throughout the country bears evidence of a greater force at work and requires more than just individual recipes for its correction. Consider the

---

4. Ibid.
5. Clarke, "Paul Robeson," 189.

idea that the Civil Rights Movement was just under sixty short years ago. The notion that four hundred years of oppression, discrimination, and exclusion from mainstream society can be wiped away in such a short period is simply a fallacy. For this reason Dr. King, a champion of colorblindness, realized that the nation could not move forward without a "Disenfranchised Bill of Rights" in order to address the poverty present in our nation. For him, America could not achieve his racial dream without some level of retribution to address injustices of the past. In order to move beyond the racial demons, a full assessment of the complex history of race in America is necessary.

Toward this end, America must also move beyond the patronizing celebration of tokenism that so commonly surrounds African American achievement. When this nation gives an inordinate amount of attention to stories about two African American coaches leading teams in the Super Bowl, or a person of color becoming president, it represents a form of white superiority. Broadcasting their achievements is not just a celebration of racial progress, but also a subtle reminder that people of color may not be as inferior as their collective lack of comparable achievement suggests. It is an affirmation that these people are capable, contributing, and competent citizens. For some this is a shock, for others an affirmation. However, the result is a culture that reinforces racial differences. Because the racist American leadership of the past handed down the idea that people of color were incapable of great achievement,[6] we shouldn't give weight and validity to their ideas by reacting when African Americans achieve significant milestones. This is especially true when they are achieving feats European Americans have been achieving for years. America's obsession with the novelty of minority achievement is both patronizing and insulting. Rather we ought to be ashamed that America has excluded and marginalized this group so substantially that they represent much of this nation's underclass, and have yet to reach the levels of collective achievement of European groups.

---

6. Thomas Jefferson in his 1781 book *Notes on the State of Virginia* articulated this assumed inferiority.

The Way Out

Our celebration of various African Americans being the "first" in their chosen fields fails to contribute to the racial progress it pretends to celebrate. Globally, there are examples of people of all ethnicities displaying success in a variety of professional endeavors. It is simply that when minorities achieve in fields in which they were previously denied access they become both heroes and spectacles. If we understood that true equality is self-evident and that racism, rather than racial differences, is to blame for obvious disparities, our collective responses would be different. America ought not to honor its historic inequality through patronizing gestures. While this treatment fuels pride among successful African Americans, it simultaneously fuels superiority among European Americans as this achievement is seen as the exception rather than the norm. This phenomenon is further evidenced by the disturbing use of terms like "poor white trash." This term is reflective of the superiority dynamic as it assumes that the majority of European Americans are respectable, while this particular group is relegated to the status of suffering the same ills as the minority American underclass. There is no "poor black trash" nor "poor Latino trash" terminology because the assumption is their collective inadequacy. America must both admit the prevalence of this psyche and openly and comprehensively address its falsehood in order to transform our national conversation on race.

For this reason, I am reticent to join in celebrations of tokenism whether they focus on accomplishments in sports, politics, science, business, or popular culture. Although some celebrate the toppling of barriers to achievement, let us rather focus our collective energies on challenging the institutions that perpetuate racism. This will ultimately prove more fruitful than joining in the media's awe surrounding the ability of individuals and the subsequent distancing of them from other members of their ethnic group. Tokenism is detrimental. With respect to the issue of recognizing human achievement, ignoring race represents the only true promoter of equality. When all Americans have an equal possibility of success and race becomes a secondary or nonexistent component in its analysis, we will have achieved true racial progress.

Unfortunately, there are divided ideologies surrounding the issue of race that are largely based on ethnic identity, social class, and life experiences. Many European Americans believe that racism is no longer a problem. A recent Tufts University survey showed that "Both whites and blacks agree that anti-black racism has decreased over the last 60 years. However, whites believe that anti-white racism has increased and is now a bigger problem than anti-black racism. Blacks, however, reported only a modest increase in their perceptions of 'reverse racism'.[7] In this way, both groups currently claim victimhood. African Americans largely perceive themselves as the target of systematic institutional racism and bias. Equally, European Americans now see themselves as suffering from policies designed to rectify past injustices. These differences in perspective are evident in the faith community as well.

James Meeks, a Chicago pastor and former Illinois State Senator, articulates a clear distinction between the African and European American faith community. He states that "white evangelicals are opposed to social programs, think most black poverty is self-imposed, and would rather plan than do. 'The religious tools that [white] evangelicals use are completely individualistic,'" Meeks said. "'There are no social problems, there are only problems with individuals. . . . But for black evangelicals, there are, and that's a fundamental difference. It can be seen as a theological difference as well.'"[8] There are clearly two separate realities for the two groups of people. Rather than ignoring this truth and operating from a spirit of accusation and partisanship, Americans must respect and learn from the differing perspectives in order to move forward. Both have validity. African Americans must operate as though racism and discrimination are not insurmountable barriers, recognizing the tremendous opportunities that the United States provides. European Americans must understand that America, despite its promise of equality for generations of people, has never achieved this for large segments of the population. While many strides have been made in this country, the residual effects of slavery will not

---

7. "Whites Believe They Are Victims."
8. Joyce, "Evangelical Rainbow Attack."

disappear overnight. America cannot turn a blind eye to the concomitant realities of universal opportunity and institutional disadvantage. This approach represents a realistic assessment of both the strengths and weaknesses of the nation while promoting progress for all segments of society. While we cannot allow America to forget the past, we must reject the notion that our separate viewpoints on issues of race will forever prevent us from coalescing around a set of common-sense solutions. Given this assessment, there is much work to be done by members of both ethnic groups in order to address the scars of the past and move towards a place of healing, understanding, and mutual prosperity. Language is an important place to begin.

Language

For both African Americans and European-Americans, healing the racial divide and countering years of white supremacist thought means changing the language that we use. While most conversations about racial language often focus on universally understood offensive terminology, there are more commonly used terms whose use is equally problematic. They are the words "black" and "white." In the English language, these terms represent the antithesis of one another. Where blackness exists, whiteness cannot. Where whiteness exists, blackness cannot. Here are just some of the definitions of the word "black" according to Webster's dictionary.

1. soiled or stained with dirt: That shirt was black within an hour.
2. gloomy; pessimistic; dismal: a black outlook.
3. deliberately; harmful; inexcusable: a black lie.
4. boding ill; sullen or hostile; threatening: black words; black looks.
5. without any moral quality or goodness; evil; wicked: His black heart has concocted yet another black deed.
6. indicating censure, disgrace, or liability to punishment: a

black mark on one's record.

7. marked by disaster or misfortune: black areas of drought; Black Friday.
8. wearing black or dark clothing or armor: the black prince.
9. based on the grotesque, morbid, or unpleasant aspects of life: black comedy; black humor.
10. illegal or underground: The black economy pays no taxes.
11. deliberately false or intentionally misleading: black propaganda.
12. British. boycotted, as certain goods or products by a trade union.

And the word "white":
1. of the color of pure snow, of the margins of this page, etc.; reflecting nearly all the rays of sunlight or a similar light.
2. Slang. decent, honorable, or dependable: That's very white of you.
3. auspicious or fortunate.
4. morally pure; innocent.
5. without malice; harmless: white magic.[9]

Both terms clearly represent a set of assumptions that are damaging when attached to ethnic groups. Americans would do well to consider a new nomenclature. For years, Americans have wrestled with terminology surrounding this issue. According to Dr. Cornel West in his book *Race Matters*, "Without the presence of black people in America, European-Americans would not be "white"—they would be Irish, Italians, Poles, Welsh, and other engaged in class, ethnic, and gender struggles over resources and identity."[10] The designation of a people as collectively "white" is an American phenomenon born in a culture of racial subjugation.

---

9. *Dictionary.com Unabridged*, s.v. "black" and "white."
10. West, Race Matters, 107–8.

The Way Out

African Americans have been called "Negro," "colored," "niggers," "niggas," "black," "Afro-Americans," and "people of color." Most common in current conversations, we refer to people of African descent as "black" and those of European decent as "white." Why? These terms, in addition to being inaccurate, do a great deal to further polarize and oversimplify the differences between us. Consider for a moment the fact that the color black is the polar opposite of the color white. Consider also that in the English language the word "black" has explicitly evil and morally defunct connotations and the word "white" assumes superiority and moral goodness. No other group in this country is referred to in the same way. If someone were to walk up to an Asian person and refer to them as the "yellow," or a Native American and refer to them as the "red," or a Latino and refer to them as "brown," it would be considered insulting. Additionally, these limited color-based notions of ethnicity are completely inaccurate. There are no truly black people in the world, nor truly white people. There are a variety of people of various skin tones including brown, tan, peach, etc. However, there are no people on the planet with truly black or white skin. Consequently, in addition to being insulting, polarizing, and relatively racist, these terms are also erroneous. We must change the terminology we use with respect to racial groups if we desire to change the relationships we have with one another. While racial issues in the United States may be much larger than language, we know that words matter. If this were not so, why would the federal government identify a variety of terms that represent hate speech, and subsequently fail to receive First Amendment protections? Language is a significant part of the legacy of racial injustice in this nation. Progress requires us to alter it.

With this in mind, America should also embrace a new approach to racial classification that is consistent, culturally sensitive, and accurate. If we view geography as an equalizer, and primarily promote the commonality of all Americans, it makes sense to therefore call ourselves American Africans, American Europeans, and American Asians rather than using the tired labeling of the past. I promote the future use of the term "American" first as recognition of a shared nationality. However, using a continental descriptor as a secondary term pays homage a person's ethnic origin and respects current cultural and ethnic differences. We are all Americans, yet have shared ancestry with groups from a variety of international locations. Rather than attempting to address every detail of historic and current national identity issues, relegating this label to a collective continent would provide for consistency and account for the lack of specific national identities for African Americans that resulted from the slave trade. It would also account for changes in national borders and identities that inevitably have occurred on every continent throughout history. This new labeling will assist Americans in moving towards a common national identity while recognizing past origins. This seems to be the fairest model for transforming a current racial lexicon that refers to some groups by national or continental identity and others by colors. While this may reflect a significant paradigm shift in thinking about race, it is time for this nation to begin the hard work of true racial maturation.

Racial Classification

Furthermore, we must address our national criterion for classifying people into perceived existing ethnic groups. America has a long history of using these often arbitrary and inconsistent standards to promote inequality through racial separation. The most egregious example of this may be the creation of the "one-drop rule." Based on a number of state statutes including Virginia's 1924 Racial Integrity Act, this rule legally defined "blackness" as having one parent or grandparent of African descent. It guaranteed that millions of biracial Americans would be classified as "black" and consequently would be restricted from many of America's legal and social benefits. Furthermore, it gave legal structure and support to the American eugenics movement, which promoted the use of segregation, forced sterilization, and abortion to assure racial purity. The "one-drop rule" facilitated this movement by creating a permanent and separate underclass of Americans who were considered tainted because of their partial Negro ancestry.

The Way Out

This law applies to no other group in American culture and has no real international precedence. "Whiteness" had similar cultural inconsistencies. In fact, the U.S. Supreme Court changed the definition of "whiteness" on several occasions. This is first seen in the 1922 case *Ozawa v. The United States*, in which a Japanese resident of California was denied naturalization because the court ruled that he wasn't "white." The court justified this ruling based on geographic definitions of the term "Caucasian" and a 1790 statute that restricted naturalization to "free white men." According to them, Ozawa was not Caucasian because Japan did not classify as a nation from which Caucasians descended. Therefore, he was denied the benefits and legal protections of American citizenship.

The very next year, in *Thind v. The United States*, the same court changed the basis for its previous ruling when faced with an Indian man who was classified as Caucasian based on his nationality. Technically, India was considered by anthropologists to be a nation from which Caucasians descended. However, the court decided that in this case "Caucasian" did not equal "white" and consequently Mr. Thind was denied citizenship. The court ruled that "whiteness" is based on the average man's opinion, as "the average man knows perfectly well that there are unmistakable and profound differences." They further argued that racial difference was "a matter of familiar observation and knowledge" and was "of such character and extent that the great body of our people instinctively recognize it and reject the thought of assimilation."[11] Mr. Thind could not be classified as "white" essentially because he didn't look the part. The result was a subjective, inconsistent, and malleable definition of "whiteness" that culturally remains today.

Of course, neither the definition of "whiteness" nor of "blackness" holds consistently outside of the United States. Various parts of the world have adopted different systems of classification for this same phenomenon. In Brazil, for instance, there are cultural assumptions about race that essentially represent the antithesis of the one-drop rule. "According to Jose Neinstein, a native white Brazilian and executive director of the Brazilian-American Cultural

---

11. *United States v. Bhagat Singh Thind*, 261 U.S. 204 (1923).

Institute in Washington, in the United States, 'If you are not quite white, then you are black.' However, in Brazil, 'If you are not quite black, then you are white.' Neinstein recalls talking with a man of Sydney Poitier's [dark] complexion when in Brazil: 'We were discussing ethnicity, and I asked him, 'What do you think about this from your perspective as a black man?' He turned his head to me and said, 'I'm not black,' . . . It simply paralyzed me. I couldn't ask another question."[12] For many years in Caribbean islands like Grenada, those who were classified as biracial, or mulattos, were a clear and distinct ethnic group from those who were either slaves or slave owners. Their mixed identity created a new social and racial class.

Furthermore, according to work done by Dr. Henry Louis Gates, "fully 58 percent of African Americans have at least 12.5 percent European ancestry,"[13] the equivalent of one great-grandparent. A similar study suggests that though possibly more distant, at least 30 percent of European Americans have one African ancestor.[14] This research suggests that the four-hundred-year American history of cultural integration has eviscerated assumptions of racial demarcations. Why is all of this relevant? America's overgeneralization of racial classifications has exacerbated the supposed differences between American racial groups and the assumed points of demarcation. America has a history of arbitrary and inconsistent lines that are increasingly proving to be erroneous. Racial identity in the United States is largely subjective. Unfortunately, our culture has not understood this reality and continues the simplistic assessments of the past. While current cultural examples abound, the most trenchant reflection of this mentality is President Barack Obama's classification as a "black" man. Being the son of a Kenyan man and a European American woman, Obama is the quintessential example of a biracial American. America still, however, strictly classifies him as "black," and expects him to view the world through that lens. As a result of our aforementioned history, having one parent of African descent negates the influence of his mother in

---

12. Fears, "People of Color."
13. Gates, "Shared Ancestries Revealed."
14. Sailer, "Race Now: Part 2."

America's collective view. Even with a mother of European descent who raised him with her family in Indonesia and Hawaii, he is considered the representative of African Americans. His presidency provides America the chance to embrace a shared racial identity. He represents Americans of both European and African ancestry. The uniqueness of his identity could have connected disparate groups and address a history of division. Yet the occurrence of African Americans claiming him as theirs and European Americans feeling threatened by his African ancestry has caused us to miss this unique historic opportunity. Disappointingly, we may not see the same opportunity for generations.

In order to move beyond America's racial demons and to truly grasp the goal of racial equality, it is time for a fresh approach to the issue of race in America. The future prosperity of African Americans and all Americans depends on it. This new approach should fully recognize the travesties of the past in their entirety. It benefits no group to ignore history or diminish its impact on the present condition of millions of Americans. America's obvious racial disparities cannot be reduced either to a collective lack of individual responsibility or to an amalgamation of poor moral choices. While poor decisions may account for some of the lack of progress for people of African descent, they cannot explain away hundreds of years of slavery and discrimination that ended less than one hundred years ago. This kind of ill-informed and myopic view of history does little to move us forward and further exacerbates the gap that exists between the ethnic groups of this nation.

Consider the complex example of the Israeli-Palestinian relationship. While I support the Israeli claim to many disputed territories, it is difficult to not empathize with the disaffected Palestinian people. Many, especially the young, face high unemployment, deep segregation, and bleak prospects for prosperity. "Almost a third of the 4.2 million Palestinians in the West Bank and Gaza are between 15 and 29 years old, and a third of this youth bulge have no jobs and scant opportunity to challenge their own aging leaders, let alone

Israel's occupation, beyond taking to the streets."[15] Their social and economic isolation fuels deviant behavior. Like potential gang members in cities like Chicago, these youth are easily recruited for violence. They often see participation in violent groups like Al-Qaeda as preferable to their current existence. Consequently, we must advocate solutions that take the social realities of disaffected groups into account. Millions still struggle with poverty, violence, and despair. Changing the social conditions in which many African American youth are reared will do much to change their shared behavior.

Simultaneously, we cannot excuse miscreant behavior for the sake of being understanding.

The United States provides tremendous opportunities for African Americans and other groups. It is equally damaging to ignore the present possibilities for individual achievement because of a focus on collective oppression. African Americans cannot be relegated to a group identity that solely defines them in light of discrimination and systematic racism. The beauty of the American experience is that this collective reality has not existed for millions of young minorities in this nation. Many fail to view themselves through a single racial lens, as their wealthy or middle class status has afforded them the ability to see America for what it can be, not strictly for what it is not. I am a product of this kind of upbringing as my parents were able to give me the kind of life that was the envy of many of my friends of all ethnicities. This included European vacations, country club membership, private education, and a family business that afforded consistent access to job opportunities. I cannot view America strictly through the lens of oppression as I see my destiny as controlled primarily by my own decisions rather than outside forces. It is vital to recognize the heterogeneity of thought and experience within every ethnic group. A 2007 poll by the Pew Research Center shows that nearly 40 percent of low-income African Americans say they have nothing in common with their middle-income counterparts.[16] The Millennial generation is redefining

---

15. "Frustrated Palestinian Youth."

16. Steve Inskeep and Juan Williams, Poll Education, Income Segregates Blacks, NPR, November 14, 2007, http://www.npr.org/templates/story/story.php?storyId=16281886.

America's understanding of race and the economic assumptions that are attached to it. Their experiences are vastly different. African American students now represent 14 percent of all graduating college graduating seniors in the U.S., according to *The 4th Annual AP Report to the Nation* (College Board, 2008).[17] The number of those being educated has finally reached their representative percentage in the population. These young African Americans will view and shape the world in different ways than their predecessors.

Consequently, even in the midst of great collective struggle, there also exists a different reality for millions of African Americans. The assumption that ethnic identity is immutably connected to a perspective of economic depravity and struggle is a false one. Our new understanding of race should reflect the full spectrum of the aforementioned experiences.

New generations of Americans from all ethnicities view race through a different lens than their parents and grandparents. Their experiences will significantly alter future political and social conversations on this issue. Those members of either major political ideology whose rhetoric only serves to simplify the challenges and amplify current tensions are dangerous and should be rejected. We must work together, embracing our mutual responsibilities while remaining hopeful for the future. Though change is never simple, we must move forward. As Abraham Lincoln reminded us during his famous 1858 speech, "a house divided against itself cannot stand."[18] Our prospects for prosperity are interwoven. Americans need one another. The sense of mutual obligation and shared destiny in the area of race relations will produce a future significantly brighter than our past. I look forward to this future.

---

17. Malik S. Henfield, Ahmad R. Washington, and Delila Owens, "To Be or Not to Be Gifted," *Gifted Child Today*, spring 2010, vol. 32 no. 2, p. 18. http://www.rodneytrice.com/sfbb/articles/gifted.pdf (accessed June 20, 2013).

18. Lincoln, "'A House Divided.'"

3

Rejecting a Depraved Culture

The Fourth Great Awakening will be: fueled by a revulsion with what believers see as the corruption of contemporary society . . . [a rebellion] against sexual debauchery, against indulgence in alcohol, tobacco, gambling, and drugs, against gluttony, and against all other forms of self-indulgence that titillate the senses and destroy the soul.

—Robert W. Fogel, economist, University of Chicago[1]

In biology, culture is defined as the product of cultivating living material. In another way, the word culture is defined as "a particular stage of civilization that defines a nation or a people."[2]

When future historians look back at the civilization in which we live, they will examine our culture. They will review artifacts, language, music, literature, and theater. They will gain their understanding of the people that lived during this time not as much from their political and economic structures but from their way of life. Subsequently, the question that must be asked is: what do current cultural customs and mores say about this generation?

---

1. Fogel, *Fourth Great Awakening*, 18.
2. *Dictionary.com Unabridged*, s.v. "culture."

The Way Out

In many ways, there are a myriad of achievements of which to be proud in the African American community. The election of Barack Obama, the large number of people who have overcome discrimination and a history of slavery to move into the middle and upper class of this nation, and the powerful spiritual and cultural traditions that have been forged through history are all examples of incredible leaps of progress of which to be proud. Yet simultaneously there exist large incarceration rates, out-of-wedlock birthrates, and murder rates. While the reasons for the aforementioned truths are multifaceted, probity, virtue, and ethical values all are vital in discussing feasible solutions.

The materialism, sexual immorality, excessive consumption, unhealthy lifestyle choices, selfishness, and the celebration of miscreant behaviors that have ravaged American society as a whole have had a more significant impact on African Americans. Consequently, one of the greatest enemies and impediments to success is the destruction brought about by a culture devoid of clear and consistent moral law. In reference to economic hardship, it is often said that when America catches a cold, African Americans catch pneumonia. This is also very true in the area of American morality. When one views some of the most deplorable aspects of American culture, African Americans are often ardent supporters, contributors, and willing participants at their own peril. The promiscuity and materialism encouraged by popular music, tragic shows about infidelity like *The Jerry Springer Show*, the celebration of marijuana use, and an exploitive and narcissistic culture of reality television all work against our collective advancement.

The impact of these trends has been devastating for communities of color. Every major indicator of the social health and stability of a population is reflective of this destruction. African Americans consistently suffer from high levels of violence, out-of-wedlock births, STD transmission, drug use, unemployment, and poverty. For the sake of rejecting the oversimplification of the issues, I do acknowledge the role of not only individual behavior and public policy decisions, but also the European American dominated media that makes these examples possible. And while full responsibility for this does not rest with the media, its continual promotion of sexually gratifying and materialistic imagery is a major part of the problem. The profit-driven media promotes a depraved popular culture because it appeals to America's lowest common cultural denominator. Without the leadership of this group there would be no platform for these cases. However, communities of color willingly give these exploiters plenty of material with which to work. There can be no discussion of progress without a rejection of this popular deviant culture.

American young people of all ages increasingly reflect an ethically compromised environment of violence, drug use, and sexual promiscuity. Consider the following studies:

> The Report Card on the Ethics of American Youth found that 92 percent of the 8,600 students surveyed lied to their parents in the past year. Seventy-eight percent said they had lied to a teacher, and more than one in four said they would lie to get a job.
>
> Nearly one in six students said they had shown up for class drunk at least once in the past year. Sixty-eight percent admitted they hit someone because they were angry. Nearly half—47 percent—said they could get a gun if they wanted to.[3]

In 2008, University of Notre Dame sociologist Christian Smith conducted a study of 230 18–23-year-olds around the issue of morality. His work was concerned with determining young adults' perceptions of society's most important moral issues. "When asked to describe a moral dilemma they had faced, two-thirds of the young people either couldn't answer the question or described problems that are not moral at all, like whether they could afford to rent a certain apartment or whether they had enough quarters to feed the meter at a parking spot." His book, *Lost in Translation*, paints a picture of a generation wholly unconcerned with greater moral questions and committed to individuality so heavily that collective morality is rejected as oppressive and limiting. *New York Times columnist David Brooks writes about this phenomenon saying*, "In most times and in most places, the group was seen to be

---

3. Durham, "Study: Teen Morality."

the essential moral unit. A shared religion defined rules and practices. Cultures structured people's imaginations and imposed moral disciplines. But now more people are led to assume that the free-floating individual is the essential moral unit. Morality was once revealed, inherited and shared, but now it's thought of as something that emerges in the privacy of your own heart."[4]

This shift in values has not just impacted younger people as adults display the same level of moral ambiguity. In the midst of these ethical challenges most Americans recognize their implications yet remain conflicted about adhering to consistent standards. A study about American morality revealed that "More than four out of five adults—83 percent—contend that they are concerned about the moral condition of the nation. Given that 84 percent of all adults consider themselves to be Christian; they have good reason to worry about the moral state of the country: many of their own views conflict with the moral teachings of their professed faith."

Of the various moral behaviors evaluated,

> a majority of Americans believed that a number of activities were "morally acceptable." Those included gambling (61percent) and co-habitation (60 percent). Nearly half of the adult population felt that two other behaviors were morally acceptable: having an abortion (45percent) and having a sexual relationship with someone of the opposite sex other than their spouse (42 percent). About one-third of the population gave the stamp of approval to pornography (38 percent), profanity (36 percent), drunkenness (35 percent) and homosexual sex (30 percent).[5]

America's moral complexities can be largely attributed to an ideological landscape heavily influenced by postmodernism. Postmodernism, with its emphasis on relativistic approaches to morality, has ravaged the moral lives of Americans of all ethnicities. It has stressed that the highest moral value is acceptance and the avoidance of judgment. Along with the European Enlightenment influence, which stressed the notion of human autonomy—that every

---

4. Brooks, "If It Feels Right . . ."
5. Barna Group, "Morality Continues to Decay."

person should have the ability to create his own moral standards—these ideological forces have guided American moral thought for centuries. Capitalism and its subsequent focus on self-pleasing consumerism have further exacerbated the problem of immorality in the nation.

The resulting impact on American culture has been the prioritization of individualism and an ever-present sense of moral ambiguity that plagues much of the nation. While I do not believe that African American youth are any more immoral than others, I am convinced that these behaviors have more destructive consequences in communities that are already suffering greatly. With the nation's highest abortion rates, out of wedlock childbirth rates, and rates of violence, urban minority communities can ill afford to participate in these trends.

And while African Americans suffer from the aforementioned ethical crisis, it is clear that current trends are not consistent with the historic West African ethos. West African cultural traditions provide great insight into African Americans' moral ancestry. "*Iwa* (character) is, for the Yoruba, 'perhaps the most important moral concept. A person is morally evaluated according to his/her *iwa*—whether good or bad' (Gbadegesin, 1991: 79). African ethics is, thus, a character-based ethics that maintains that the quality of the individual's character is most fundamental in our moral life."[6] Additionally, community shares equal importance.

"In Akan moral thought, the notion is expressed most vividly in an art motif that shows a 'siamese' crocodile with two heads but a single (i.e., common) stomach. The common stomach of the two crocodiles indicates that at least the basic interests of all the members of the community are identical. It can therefore be interpreted as symbolizing the *common good*, the good of all the individuals within a society."[7] Both character and community are traditionally important to West Africans. In fact this community, along with many around the world, provides various forms of collective sanctions for those who reject these principles. For this reason, West

---

6. Gyekye, "African Ethics."
7. Ibid.

The Way Out

Africa's descendants would do well to re-embrace these principles and rebuff notions of materialism and individualism that are common in current American culture. No amount of outside intervention can ever replace this needed revolution in values and beliefs so critical to the African American community.

My father and mother understood this commitment to morality, family, and community. Like many who faced non-ideal economic and even relational circumstances, they could have easily made different choices. My mother turned down significant career advancement during her life to protect our family's delicate structure. In many similar circumstances parents make decisions to pursue their own happiness at the expense of their children's well-being. This culture is prevalent today, although it has shifted significantly even in the time I have been alive. Even a few decades ago, African Americans had not fully embraced deleterious cultural trends like out-of-wedlock births. The biggest difference between the 1970s, when I was born, and now is that my father would still have been shunned socially for a decision to absolve himself of his responsibility. This dynamic has changed. Culturally, there existed an expectation that a father was to take care of his children, regardless of any personal challenges this brought for both people. Often times this meant marriage, but not always. Sometimes it meant simply extending financial support. For my father it meant a commitment to marriage. Thankfully for me, it allowed me to have a father in my life who served as a role model and mentor. I often wonder what my life would have been like had he chosen the path that so many young men today have chosen to take. My parents, though they struggled through many challenges, persevered in their relationship for the sake of my brother and myself. Had either of them given up on the ideal of family for the sake of personal gratification and expediency, my life would have taken a decidedly negative turn. I prospered because of their decisions. Sadly, the vast majority of African American children today will have a dissimilar experience.

The Romans

The United States has often been compared ancient to Rome. These comparisons are vast, specifically in the areas of military conquest, political structure, and extreme wealth inequality. However, the most significant areas of comparison are morality, infidelity, homosexuality, infanticide, prostitution, materialism, greed, and a glorification of violence. These were all highly common in Roman culture and are equally common in the US. In his book *Twilight of a Great Civilization*, author Carl F. H. Henry describes Rome as a place where barbarism, based on a pagan moral culture and the absence of fixed truth, was the dominant ideology of the day. Author Carl Wilson, in his book *Our Dance Has Turned to Death*, further explains this picture. He describes Rome through a set of societal patterns in stages of decline. This decline includes a culture in which spiritual and moral development became secondary to materialistic pursuits, male homosexuality was celebrated, violence was a typical form of entertainment, and fidelity in marriage became uncommon. Furthermore, the exaltation of individuality juxtaposed with various forms of pagan worship created a society in which individual morality was de-emphasized. The Christian historical text *We Don't Speak Great Things, We Live Them* depicts an ancient Roman environment in which both abortion and infanticide through a variety of methods were widespread as well.[8]

The U.S., in its promotion of relativistic morality, individualism, and sexual liberation, has rejected the important countervailing principles of moral consistency and absolutism, community, and sexual fidelity. In 2002, *U.S. News and World Report* cited a Zogby International poll, commissioned by the National Association of Scholars, of 401 randomly selected college seniors. In this poll, 73 percent of the students indicated that they were taught by professors who substituted uniform standards of right and wrong for a commitment to tolerance, diversity, and relativism. This major and recent cultural shift threatens the foundations of a free society whose survival depends on a consistent, collective, and self-constraining moral ethos. Many of the founding fathers recognized

---

8. Justin Martyr and Felix, *We Don't Speak Great Things*.

this. The second President of the United States, John Adams, said, "The constitution was made for a moral and religious people. For the governance of any other, it is wholly inadequate." George Washington, in his 1796 Farewell Address to the nation, called religion and morality "indispensible supports" of "political prosperity." Moreover, he was concerned about attempting to sustain national morality without religion as its chief guide. "Whatever may be conceded to the influence of refined education on minds of peculiar structure, reason and experience both forbid us to expect that national morality can prevail in exclusion of religious principle."[9] He warned Americans about accepting the kind of ethereal and non-specific morality that is so common today. Both gentlemen, along with many of the nation's framers, recognized the potential instability of a society built on mutable and secular definitions of morality. They recognized that this phenomenon would require the government to play a greater role in the lives of its citizens. Freedom itself is predicated upon the notion that individuals have the ability to be self-governing and can erect moral boundaries to protect them from the destruction of themselves and others. For the nation's founders, this was the only path to survival for a free society. As we can clearly see, our nation's current incarceration rates (we have the largest prison population in the world) and heavy dependence on government social services (the nation's largest employer is the federal government) to counter deficiencies in individual and family behavior are clear results of this dynamic. Leaders of every community must understand the crucial role that faith can play in assisting the nation in solving some of its most severe dilemmas. Yet much of America's current culture sees religion's role as ancillary at best, and as antithetical to American progress at worst. Unfortunately these leaders have no alternate answer to changing the culture of selfishness and irresponsibility that is at the core of issues like violence, the out-of-wedlock birthrate, and drug/alcohol use. Unless leaders recognize this truth, they are in danger of working to destroy the very nation they claim to defend. As Washington reminded us about religion and morality, "In vain would that man

---

9. Washington, *Farewell Address*, 105.

claim the tribute of patriotism, who should labor to subvert these great pillars of human happiness, these firmest props of the duties of men and citizens. The mere politician, equally with the pious man, ought to respect and to cherish them."[10]

I recently had a conversation with a relative who had a child out of wedlock. He is a young man, uninterested in the restrictions that come from married life. While he desires marriage in the future, he feels that at age twenty he wants to enjoy his young life. This would all be acceptable were it not for the fact that another life is dependent upon him for direction, nourishment, and stability. My relative is an unfortunate product of the current culture in this nation. The self-consumed message of American life unfortunately places the happiness of adults above the well-being of children. We see this in a variety of areas that include divorce laws and redefinitions of marriage that are strictly based on procuring adult pleasure with little thought to their greater impact on children. It is culturally acceptable for sex and relationships to be strictly based on personal pleasure detached from their greater social function. It is acceptable to seek individual fulfillment at all cost. Regrettably, it is our children who bear the burden for these decisions.

A Collective Focus

During the Civil Rights Movement, it was often said that African Americans represented the moral conscience of our nation. It was said that African Americans encouraged Americans to transcend their myopic self-interests and remember a larger set of moral obligations to one another. Given our current moral climate, with our irreverent popular culture and watered-down religious teachings on personal righteousness, we are desperately in danger of losing this position. This problem is greater than any economic crisis, any educational inequalities, or any discriminatory policies that exist. America's spiritual house is on fire, and we need leaders who understand both the urgency and depth of this challenge.

---

10. Ibid., 136.

The Way Out

The collective morality of the nation must rise above individualistic pursuits based on moral relativism. This is especially important for African Americans. Even in a nation where there exist great opportunities for economic and social advancement, our pursuits must strike a greater chord.

Political involvement for its own sake is worthless. In the same, way scholarship and even artistic proficiency are worthless if not tied to the greater theme. There is a proper place for all pursuits. The unfortunate emphasis on athletics and entertainment as the chief tool for social mobility for millions of African American males represents an example of misplaced priorities. In 1903 President Theodore Roosevelt wrote a letter to his son about this very matter. Roosevelt, a president with a great reputation for sportsmanship, told him that he was delighted to have him play sports and that he believed in them greatly. However, he warned him:

> but I do not believe in them if they degenerate into the sole end of any one's existence. I don't want you to sacrifice standing well in your studies to any over-athleticism; and I need not tell you that character counts for a great deal more than either intellect or body in winning success in life. Athletic proficiency is a mighty good servant, and like so many other good servants, a mighty bad master. Did you ever read Pliny's letter to Trajan, in which he speaks of its being advisable to keep the Greeks absorbed in athletics, because it distracted their minds from all serious pursuits, including soldiering, and prevented their ever being dangerous to the Romans? . . . A man must develop his physical prowess up to a certain point; but after he has reached that point there are other things that count more.
>
> He goes on to praise his son's athletic ability in the areas of football and boxing, but reminds him, "But don't ever get into the frame of mind which regards these things as constituting the end to which all your energies must be devoted, or even the major portion of your energies."[11]

This warning is essential for all young Americans, specifically those of color. An overwhelming number of young people see

---

11. Roosevelt, "Proper Place for Sports," in *Theodore Roosevelt's Letters*.

sports and entertainment as the sole option for transcending their economically depraved conditions. Our ability to excel collectively will depend on developing a correct sense of prioritization. According to Roosevelt, the Greeks were overtaken and proved less of a threat because of their collective distractions. While America fails to see these pursuits as distractions, successful nations have historically understood the need for proper national focus. Principles like scholarship, ingenuity, and entrepreneurship, when connected to a greater national mission, have the ability to transform the world. Furthermore, African Americans would benefit greatly from this approach.

African Americans, like many Americans, have fallen into the pit of being distracted by the pursuit of pleasure. Nowhere is this more obvious than in the area of entertainment.

The popularity of reality television, sexually explicit and exploitive talk shows, vulgar forms of comedy, and violent films speak to the cultural depravity facing the nation. Unfortunately, African Americans are willing participants in these forms of entertainment. However, even when most Americans decide to reject portions of this culture, unfortunately it is replaced strictly with additional monetary pursuits. Yet the pursuit of money only contributes to the "pleasure principle," as its ultimate goal is strictly worry-free living. Financial stability is a laudable goal. However, when human beings are reduced to self-sustenance and preservation as their foremost mission in life, they become little more than animals. Is this not what animals do? No animal is going to put any pursuit above self-preservation. It is instinctual. Many may argue that it is instinctual for us as well. Yet in the human race, the few individuals that are able to transcend this instinct and live for others are considered remarkable. People like Dr. Martin Luther King Jr., Mother Theresa, Nelson Mandela, and Ghandi are praised because their most significant accomplishments uplifted all of humanity rather than simply themselves. Dr. King was convinced of this fact. "An individual has not started living until he can rise above the narrow confines of his individualistic concerns to the broader concerns of all humanity."[12]

12. King, "Remaining Awake."

Greatness as achieved through the pursuit of the collective good has the potential to transform both individuals and communities. Subsequently, the principles of delayed gratification and sacrifice have very practical life changing consequences for poor communities. Consider that 78 out of every 100 professional NFL players are bankrupt within three years of retirement despite earning tens of millions, or in some cases, hundreds of millions of dollars. In the NBA, the figure is 60 out of 100 that face severe financial hardship within five years of retirement. Ironically, winning the lottery if you are poor doubles your chances of bankruptcy. The conditions of poverty create an ideological subculture that must be addressed if people have a hope of overcoming it. Author Ruby Payne in *A Framework for Understanding Poverty* suggests that "poverty is caused by an entirely different worldview, and that the people who grow up in poverty are acting rationally based upon their own life experiences."[13] The author describes the priority of survival knowledge for poor people, which includes access to government programs and social/physical survival skills. This body of knowledge and behavior is much different from those who come from more affluent homes. Their survival skills may relate to finding the right mate or making the right academic choices. The result is that the more affluent a person is, the more they have the luxury of focusing on interests greater than themselves. They also have a greater understanding of issues like savings, investment, and delayed gratification.[14] If we can change the worldview of Americans who live in poverty, we can change their economic, social, and moral outcomes.

And while in America, selfless pursuits are rare, they are less rare among groups not suffering through the struggle of basic survival. The reason is clear. Collective wealth affords people the opportunity to transcend individual interests. African Americans, still predominately preoccupied with survival have not had this luxury. For example, this is why there exists a greater abundance of European American missionaries to developing nations, including

---

13. Kennon, "New Study."
14. Kennon, "Being an Effective Educator."

various countries in Africa, than people of color. Theologically, even in the Christian community, African Americans are still primarily concerned with self-preservation and prosperity. Understandably, personal needs come first. The psychologist Maslow argued that an individual can never focus on greater concerns until his primary physical needs are met. African Americans, in the aggregate, reflect this reality. Yet if simple economic survival remains the sole focus, the community will remain challenged in a variety of additional areas that ultimately impact its economic development as well. Progress must be tied to a larger good. Dr. King said, "I am not interested in power for power's sake, but I'm interested in power that is moral, that is right and that is good."[15] We must strive for moral uses of power or leaders from poor communities will simply replicate current injustices and inequalities with a different face. There are immoral, corrupt, and self-serving leaders of all ethnicities in this nation. Those from minority areas merely do more damage because their choices lead to the further exploitation of the needy people who depend on them. The proper collective ethos is necessary for true social elevation. This is the call of the hour for leaders who desire to affect the conundrum facing African Americans. A revolution in values that reclaims biblical principles and rejects the worse parts of American culture is essential. It is time to make the vital transition to a place of higher moral leadership, as the future of suffering communities depends on it.

---

15. Online: http://www.brainyquote.com/quotes/quotes/m/martinluth 141041.html.

4

The African American Church

Reclaiming a Legacy

The local church is the hope of the world, and its future rests primarily in the hands of its leaders.

—Bill Hybels, pastor of
Willow Creek Community Church[1]

I am a firm believer that the church represents the world's greatest hope for renewal. While institutions like the government can boast unparalleled financial resources, no organization on earth has the ability to move hearts, minds, and actions like religious institutions. The Christian church has made an indelible impact on the most aspects of Western civilization. The government, healthcare, education, art, and the nonprofit sector all have a long history of Christian influence. This history is based on a theological understanding of Christ calling his followers to be the "light of the world." He conveyed the reality that all of the world's conundrums, individual and collective, were at their core spiritual dilemmas. Consequently, while institutions like schools, businesses, the

1. Hybels, *Courageous Leadership*, 12.

government, and the media are vital for social change, the church is most essential. Without the internal change that churches are uniquely positioned to foster, our efforts are ultimately incomplete.

For this reason, I am extremely concerned with the state of not just the church as an institution, but the overall state of Christianity in the African American community. Currently, close to seventeen million African Americans attend church regularly through a variety of denominations. Christianity clearly has a great level of influence among African American people. African Americans attend church in greater numbers, and are more likely to feel comfortable bringing faith into their professional and civic lives. Fifty-two percent of African Americans attend church regularly, compared with 49 percent of European Americans, 41 percent of Latinos, and 29 percent of Asians.[2]

African Americans are also the most likely to self-identify as born-again Christians (59 percent, compared to a national average of 46 percent) and are the ethnic segment most likely to consider themselves Christian (92 percent, versus 85 percent nationally). Additionally, they are most likely to participate in church-related activities in a typical week (attending church services, participating in a small group, attending a Sunday school class, praying, and reading the Bible).[3]

As a result, there exists a significant and obvious irony. The collective public culture of this group, while reflecting a strong relationship to Christianity, is largely inconsistent with biblical principles. From political choices to popular entertainment, there exists a glaring disconnection between the culture of faith and the practical application of the tenets of that faith in the various sectors of African American life. While there are certain areas where the collective civic positions taken by this community are consistent with biblical text, for the most part, the major political leadership restricts this application to areas of social justice. Outside of this, the application of the Scriptures to other social issues is typically both inconsistent and considered extremely controversial.

2. Barna Group, "Church Attendance."
3. Barna Group, "How the Faith."

The Way Out

While Christianity has served as a powerful source of inspiration for African American leadership and the platform from which the Civil Rights Movement was launched, many argue that recent trends have diminished its influence. Reverend Joseph Lowery, immediate successor to Dr. King as the head of the Southern Christian Leadership Conference, said that African Americans "have let other folks take the moral high ground, when the moral high ground was ours. . . . We have deserted the good spouse of spirituality and are shacking up with the prostitute of materialism and greed. We have to have a new birth of spirituality because that is our strength."[4] The African American community in its faithful embrace of Christianity as a religion has collectively ignored large sections of the gospel message crucial to its survival. While much of America has done the same, the effect of this abandonment can be felt more heavily in communities ravished so heavily by poverty and despair.

In my many years of attending church, I have seen a clear distinction between church culture and biblical living. While no human being is perfect, there seems to be a culture of comfort that is more concerned with social elevation than with righteous living. In response to an experience of collective oppression, African American leadership has focused on one aspect of Christ's mission at the exclusion of the rest. Liberation theology, the ideology that sees Christ's primary concern as political and social advancement for oppressed groups, dominates the African American church. As a politically aware person of color, I have wrestled with this topic for years. On the one hand, I have found great inspiration in the work of Jesse Jackson, Al Sharpton, and countless other civil rights warriors. I can recall reading Rev. Jackson's book *Legal Lynching*, in which he described his intellectual and political development. He tells the story of how he recognized that Jesus' call to serve the poor could begin at the micro-level in one-on-one assistance. Yet ultimately it had to develop into addressing macro-economic policies that caused poverty throughout the world. This revelation shaped my own intellectual development tremendously. Consequently,

---

4. "State of the Black Union."

while I am deeply grateful for those who have preceded me in this struggle, I still find myself having significant disagreements.

There is a great need for the adoption of a Christian worldview that allows God, through the Scriptures, to lead this church community to specific and consistent social and political conclusions. A 1999 survey of 1,084 African American members of the Presbyterian Church showed a great lack of a comprehensive worldview. "In comparison to Hispanics and Koreans, African-Americans were less likely to hold that the Bible is authoritative in secular matters."[5] European Americans polled even lower when asked this question. The irony is clear also when realizing that the collective political voice of this group consistently conflicts with biblical text. The issue of abortion represents a trenchant example of this dynamic. While it is never explicitly mentioned in the Bible, a variety of Scriptures discuss God's relationship with the unborn. In a community that is the most religious in America, how can 90 percent of the people support a political party (Democrats) that fiercely protects the right to an abortion? There are various other examples; however, the overall issue of rights disconnected from the will of God is a modern ideal that has permeated the collective psyche of the entire American church. This phenomenon is probably best summarized in Craig Gay's book *The Way of The (Modern) World, or, Why It's Tempting to Live as If God Doesn't Exist.* "Soren Kierkegaard insisted that the characteristic depravity of the nineteenth century lay in its theoretical contempt for individual human beings and in the elevation of abstract humanistic ideals over real human existence."[6] As a result the abortion issue in the African American church has become a battle of choice and freedom over the reality of life. While I do not maintain that all Christians must arrive at the same political positions, the lack of a consistent biblical discussion on these issues is problematic. In the next chapter we will explore the question of political participation more deeply.

Moreover, how is it possible that the most heavily church-going group in America boasts some of the most significant social

---

5. African-American Members."
6. Gay, *Way of the Modern World*, 73.

dysfunction? Seventy percent of African American children grow up without a father in the home. Alcohol use, drug use, and sexually transmitted diseases are rampant. African American males, who make up 6 percent of the nation population, make up 60 percent of those in prison. A simplistic view of this question would exclusively blame either the individual or the larger societal institutions. There is enough blame to be had by all. One cannot ignore the four-hundred-year history of racism and discrimination in this nation. It has crippled the African American community in a myriad of ways. Furthermore, America still wrestles with injustice with respect to inequitable education funding, dissimilar criminal prosecution based on race and income, and civic leadership that is content to allow communities of color to be perpetually under-resourced and under-served. These factors are real and cannot be ignored in these discussions. However, this does not tell the complete story, as there is another phenomenon at work currently. There is an increasingly growing culture that rejects the biblical principles of marriage, fidelity, industry, community, and charity. For this dynamic to change, individual behaviors are critical. The government bears some level of responsibility, yet waiting for the larger society to address these issues is somewhat hopeless. Individuals and local communities must move now. We cannot wait. If any institution can ameliorate this crisis, the church can. With this in mind, I am encouraged by a number of examples.

Churches like Glenville New Life Community Church in Cleveland have led city-wide abstinence efforts in inner-city neighborhoods. This church, along with four others, has created a yearly purity rally entitled "True Love Waits." Hundreds of teenagers have taken this pledge each year in the face of cultural trends that consistently push them in the opposite direction. A study by the University of Texas at Austin found that religion and chastity pledges have "robust protective effects" on the incidences of premarital sex. Their restrictive influences may improve marital and health outcomes for young adults. "Nearly 40 percent of 15–25-year-old virgins surveyed said their primary motivation for abstinence was that it was against their religion or morals."[7] Furthermore, according to a 2010 study of 660 African American Philadelphia Public School students, abstinence-only programs resulted in a 33 percent reduction in sexual intercourse. The study, which appeared in *Archives of Pediatrics & Adolescent Medicine* and was conducted through the University of Pennsylvania, suggested this approach to be more effective at reducing STDs in inner-city youth than condom distribution programs.[8] Programs like these are essential to convincing specifically inner-city young people to pursue a different course. Every child saved is worth the effort. And while abstinence education has proven controversial in recent years, the crisis facing inner-city communities demands that we continue a variety of approaches, including those that stir political controversy. In my work, I have witnessed a number of similar programs that strive to counter the culture of sexual promiscuity from which so many of America's youth suffer. I have had the great privilege of participating in a myriad of faith-based programs, which for many youth represent the only alternative to the sexual promiscuity with which they are so often inundated. Their work is vital.

Despite arguments against abstinence education, the aforementioned examples prove that they are making a difference in the areas that need them most. In neighborhoods where most children are born out of wedlock and teen pregnancy derails the dreams of thousands of young people each year, abstinence education is an undeniable asset in the battle for the healthy development of young adults. If programs like this can prove even moderately effective, why would we not use them as models for what can be done in inner cities across the nation?

In addition to the tremendous progress made around the issue of abstinence and sexual fidelity, churches are also affecting educational outcomes for inner-city youth. In 2009 Brian D. Barrett, assistant professor in the Foundations and Social Advocacy Department at the State University of New York College at Cortland, published a study entitled "The 'Invisible Institution' and a Disappearing

---

7. Briggs, "Cleveland Churches."
8. Unger, "Researchers find Kids Say 'Yes.'"

Achievement Gap," in the journal *Religion and Education*. In this effort, Dr. Barrett finds that the achievement gap that exists between students of European and African descent was eliminated for those students who attended church often. He found that involvement in the church community proved to be a critical factor in the academic success of inner-city youth. Furthermore, in a 2010 study called "Faith in the Inner City: The Urban Black Church and Students' Educational Outcomes," published in Howard University's *Journal of Negro Education*, Barrett finds involvement in church is second only to parental involvement as a predictor of educational success for inner-city youth.

Scholars like Barret and Anthony Bradley argue that the church is uniquely effective at reaching this population for a number of reasons, including the following:

- The church can challenge parents and children to address the moral issues that undermine successful families and students.

- Black churches tend to be more socio-economically heterogeneous so at-risk youth can have regular interactions with high-achieving blacks for mentoring and role modeling.

- Black churches have intergenerational networks that invest in young people over the long term and provide regular adult reinforcement of good values.

- Churches invest money in creating scholarships for children that significantly humanizes the giving process and provides some informal accountability.[9]

An additional study from the *Journal of Negro Education* looked at 4,273 students. This study, entitled "How Religious, Social, and Cultural Capital Factors Influence Educational Aspirations of African American Adolescents," by Hussain Al-Fadhli and Thomas Kersen, sociology professors at Jackson State University, showed that religious involvement is a predictor of college success. In their work they said, "Students who attend church and believe religion is important may be more likely to interact with more adults who can

9. Bradley, "Inner City Churches."

help them with their school work and even provide guidance about their futures goals and plans." Additionally, students with an "active religious life, involved parents, and active social life have greater opportunities and choices in the future."[10]

Moreover, using a national sample of 6,795 eighth- and tenth-graders who completed *Monitoring the Future: A Continuing Study of American Youth in 2008*, this study found that Black students who participated in more religious activities and who had stronger religious convictions were more likely to report higher grades in school, had a positive self-concept, positive feelings about school, parents involved with their education, and fewer disciplinary referrals.[11]

The implications of these findings are significant. Barrett conveys a truth that many fail to understand. Strong churches contribute to strong families and vice versa. Both contribute to strong communities, as their roles in the positive socialization of young people are inextricably linked. The church community represents an essential part of changing the life conditions of millions of Americans. Recent efforts to silence its influence are extremely counterproductive.

Additionally, in the area of community development, the church's influence proves again to be imperative. Emmett D. Carson, author of *A Hand Up: Black Philanthropy and Self Help in America*, notes that 90 percent of all black giving is channeled through the church, making it the one enduring institution in low-income black communities with the ability to secure major credit.

In 1978 Allen African Methodist Episcopal Church, inspired by its ambitious pastor, Rev. Floyd H. Flake, took the first giant step in what would become a major community redevelopment campaign. Using a $10.7 million HUD grant, it built a three-hundred-unit senior citizens housing project. Over the next fifteen years, Allen Church established numerous service institutions, including a school and a multiservice center housing a prenatal and postnatal clinic. But it also became a builder of businesses, buying

---

10. Al-Fadhli and Kersen, "How Religious," 386–87.
11. Toldson and Anderson, "Role of Spirituality."

The Way Out

and rehabilitating more than fifteen boarded-up storefronts in its Queens, NY, community. Today these storefronts house a travel agency, medical and legal professional offices, a barber shop, a restaurant, a home-care agency, and a preschool.

The church's first project in 1978 was a complex for senior citizens. Since that time it has revived the surrounding community, building three hundred two-family homes and a school while running a medical clinic, drug counseling program, and a Head Start preschool. Allen's total assets add up to $92 million and at one time it was the sixth largest private-sector employer in all of Queens.

While in college, I had the privilege of working for a similar organization in New Brunswick, New Jersey. At the time called First Baptist Community Development Corporation, the Central New Jersey Community Development Corporation has accomplished similar feats. Since 1992 this organization has partnered with the government and private sector to direct millions of dollars into blighted areas targeted for building affordable housing, job training and placement, family support services, financial literacy, and foster care/adoption services. The work of the church and this affiliate organization has been so respected that its leader, Dr. DeForest B. Soaries, was appointed to be New Jersey's thirtieth Secretary of State.

Lastly, the African American church has the potential to play a major role in America's current educational reform efforts. Around the nation churches have provided mentoring, volunteer tutors, and even housing for public educational programs. Most significantly, the faith community can assuredly make its greatest contribution by engaging in the conversation surrounding the definition of a quality education. Dr. Martin Luther King Jr. said, "intelligence plus character—that is the goal of true education."[12] President Theodore Roosevelt said "that to educate a man in the mind and not the morals is to educate a menace to society."[13] Churches are uniquely positioned to transform the discussion surrounding educational reform

---

12. King, "Purpose of Education."

13. Online: http://www.brainyquote.com/quotes/quotes/t/theodorero 147876.html.

by promoting what it does best: building the moral character necessary for good citizenship.

Lutheran leaders like Johannes Bugenhagen, John Comenius, and Philipp Melanchthon were critical to establishing compulsory public education in Germany. America's earliest educational pioneers also came from the church community. From the Massachusetts Bay Colony Puritans, who established the nation's first public schools, to the founding of most of the country's first universities, the Christian influence on all areas of education is undeniable. For African Americans the Christian influence in education has been especially crucial, as numerous educational institutions have been founded specifically to serve this group. Pillar institutions like Howard University, Wilberforce, and Clark Atlanta University were founded with explicitly Christian goals. Without their contribution to equality through education, African Americans would face significantly greater academic barriers. While the church has proven imperfect, I am convinced that it still represents the greatest hope for the problems facing America's inner cities. We must continue to strengthen, empower, and equip this vital institution to do its important work. It is a major catalyst for changed lives. By changing lives, societies are changed in the process.

5

Political Engagement

Developing a New Agenda

How fortunate for governments that the people they administer don't think.

—Adolf Hitler[1]

The first Civil Rights Movement secured and protected the right to vote. The second Civil Rights Movement must focus on how to use it. African Americans, like most Americans, suffer from political ignorance and apathy, and the subsequent manipulation that comes as a result. Democratic participation in American elections has long been problematic. Nationally, voter turnout is 64 percent, while African American turnout, with the exception of Barack Obama's two presidential elections, is slightly under 60 percent.[2] In midterm elections all groups' collective participation drops to 41 percent.[3] However, empowered and sustained

---

1. Online: http://www.brainyquote.com/quotes/quotes/a/adolfhitle109950.html.
2. U.S. Census Bureau, "Voting and Registration," Table B.
3. McDonald, "2010 General Election."

participation, not simply turnout, may reflect the greatest impediment to progress. For this is what is most lacking. Most political activity in this country is shaped by well-financed interest groups with narrow and parochial agendas. Their influence circumvents that of the general population and encourages an ill-informed and uninvolved electorate that is easily manipulated by the two major political parties. Often Americans vote without knowing much more about candidates than what they have seen through media sound bites and slick advertisement. They have limited choices, biased information, and a vote that often is eclipsed by the forces of lobbyists and special interest groups. The second Civil Rights Movement must address this dilemma. This movement must turn its attention to fully engaging African Americans and all Americans to prepare for more significant and meaningful electoral participation. Moreover, in addition to these challenges, the current structure of our two-party system offers limited options for the advancement of urban communities. Unfortunately, African Americans possess an unhealthy allegiance to one of America's political parties, which serves to stifle the greater influence of their national vote. Since the 1965 no Republican has gained more than 15 percent of the African American vote.[4] There currently exists a dysfunctional marriage between African Americans and the Democratic Party. And, of course, this marriage truly represents the adage "till death do us part," as there is very little chance of separation or divorce. I am not necessarily promoting the notion that the Republicans would be a better spouse. I am suggesting, however, that competition is bound to make the agendas of both parties more reflective of the community's needs. No group is best served when its voting allegiance is predetermined. Competition is crucial. As Joseph Lowery of the Southern Christian Leadership Conference (SCLC) has stated, "One party takes us for granted, and the other just takes us."[5] Let's explore the failings of both parties in solving our most pressing social problems.

4. Bositis, "Blacks and the 2004 DNC," Table 1, p. 9.
5. "State of the Black Union."

The Way Out
Why Neither Major American Political Party Adequately Addresses the Full Spectrum of Needs Facing the African community

Republicans

The Declaration of Independence states, "We hold these Truths to be self-evident, that all Men are created equal, that they are endowed by their Creator with certain unalienable Rights, that among these are Life, Liberty, and the Pursuit of Happiness-That to secure these Rights, Governments are instituted among Men, deriving their just Powers from the Consent of the Governed."[6] America was founded on the principle of self-government. The Republican Party often uses this mantra to describe its mission and core beliefs. Yet today's Republican Party often fails to live up to its own ideology.

How can a party that so firmly promotes individual rule and low taxes on the one hand, support a multitude of set-asides and government mandates/regulations on the other? The military, senior citizens, the oil industry, the banking industry, utility companies, developers, the prison system, and countless others are beholden to the Republican Party for government set-asides. The idea that the average Republican is interested in small self-government is laughable.

Self-government in its truest form would require the Republicans ending corporate and senior welfare. It would require that the state have a minimal role in the lives of citizens. It may also require significant reductions in the size and scope of the American military.

Of course most are disinterested in all of these propositions. What the Republican Party is truly interested in is government spending that benefits their interests. In fact, the very notion that Republicans like Ron Paul and Michael Steele would take libertarian positions on the war in Afghanistan (suggesting that the US consider complete withdrawal) caused them to be ostracized,

---

6. The Declaration of Independence, online: http://www.ushistory.org/declaration/document/index.htm.

Political Engagement

mostly within their own party. The military industrial complex, aptly named so by Republican President Eisenhower, eats up close to a quarter of our federal expenditures. True libertarianism, self-government, and individual liberty would arm every citizen to protect themselves, and rely minimally on military and police involvement. The Republican Party is no more interested in small government than their adversaries on the other side of the aisle. (This is the same party that supported Bush's corporate bailout and rejected Obama's just a year later.) This party, like many political parties, desires power even at the expense of principle.

The irony of all of this is that the Republican Party doctrine, which includes business ownership, school choice, faith, and family, has the potential to serve the African American community well. Consider some of the most pressing issues facing our communities today. We are a people trapped in failing schools, sliding towards moral relativism, who own very few of the stores we patronize on a daily basis. Polls have shown that African Americans strongly support school choice in education, reject a strict separation of church and state, and desire a thriving entrepreneurial community. Additionally, the level of self-empowerment advocated by the Republican Party seems consistent with the philosophies of great African American leaders like Booker T. Washington, Marcus Garvey, and Malcolm X. Even on social questions like abortion and same-sex marriage, the African American community is among the most conservative groups in the nation. Support for same-sex marriage in this community is relatively low, as witnessed by the Proposition 8 measure in California and additional organized opposition around the nation. On the abortion question, increasing numbers of African Americans are waking up to the reality that groups like Planned Parenthood do more damage than good in poor communities. As a person that has spent years teaching and discussing these issues among African American college students, it is amazing the number of students who have embraced the pro-life movement when faced with the high number of African American abortions and the eugenics-inspired history of groups like Planned Parenthood. So what is the problem? Why do we not see a stronger conservative political movement among this group?

The Way Out

The answer is simple. African Americans would easily vote for Republicans if they were given viable options. The options provided by the Republicans are pitiful. Why would any community-minded African American have voted for the Romney/Ryan, Palin/McCain, or Bush/Cheney ticket when these campaigns showed little or no interest in their plight? These tickets spoke to rural America in a tone that served to alienate minority communities. The Republicans have done a deplorable job of connecting with communities of color, and they ignore these groups at their own peril. The current Republican Rarty, led by right-wing ideologues, has missed a great opportunity to reach out to minorities around the aforementioned issues. The party must find moderate candidates with a finger on the pulse of these communities in order to remain relevant. African Americans would be open to Republicans if they just asked us out on a date and pretended that they were interested. They have not. If the Republicans continue failing to capitalize on these political realities, their irrelevance is deserved.

Democrats

The current Democrats have a much stronger connection with communities of color. They, unlike their Republican counterparts, at least know that African Americans exist and are interested in addressing the concerns of this group. In Bill Clinton's *My Life*, he refers to a Goldman Sachs executive who made a decision to support him by becoming a Democrat. His rationale was that the Democrats had a heart but no head and the Republicans had a head with no heart. Since he figured that it is easier to change the heart than the mind, he chose the Democrats. Based on this perception, many African Americans have given them great allegiance. However, the tragedy of the Democrats' relationship with African Americans is that the Democratic leadership has stifled debate on the best solutions for current conundrums. African Americans who advocate any solutions outside the realm of the party platform are immediately ostracized as traitors. This lack of debate keeps an antiquated civil rights agenda in place while ignoring the changing needs and

Political Engagement

desires of the community. Ironically, the conservative voice within the community is quickly shot down, although increasing numbers of African Americans are identifying themselves as either conservative or independent. Why is it that the Democrats have the corner on the African American vote? Wouldn't it be healthier, given the capitalist principle of competition, to have varying viewpoints from which to choose? Not only would this provide different and innovative solutions, but also it would allow the current solutions to be refined and sharpened.

The African American community must abandon its blind loyalty to the Democratic Party. While our history of faith-based social activism, consistent with liberation theology, has led us to embrace much of the Democratic agenda, there are parts of that agenda that are extremely problematic. Their support for same-sex marriage, abortion, government dependency, and a secular education system and culture are inconsistent with the faith-based aspect so much a part of the African American tradition. Their rejection of school vouchers and lack of focus on entrepreneurship, business development, and family as the key to the prosperity of urban America is troubling. These Democratic policy positions are antithetical to the long-term success of African Americans. They also have often advocated for solutions that require African Americans to remain forever dependent on benevolent governmental leadership for their salvation. This is a mistake. Unfortunately, when faced with the ideological choices offered by both parties, it has been the Democratic Party's agenda that has won most often in African American circles. Dr. King warned in his book *Why We Can't Wait* that the Civil Rights Movement must retain its independence in order to remain relevant. When considered through the lens of the Christian tradition, this independence becomes even more vital. The tenets of the Christian faith inevitably lead followers to this position, as Christ's message was clearly a mixture of both major ideologies. When African Americans break free, they will force both major parties to fight for their votes, thereby guaranteeing more responsive and accountable government representation.

Most mainstream elected Democrats and Republicans have very similar positions on federal debt, senior programs, privatization, ethics in government, and foreign policy. In practice, they represent two sides of the same coin. With respect to the aforementioned issues, choosing between them really represents a set of false choices. Consequently, the major differences in the area of ideology are important. This is why controversial social issues, though polarizing, cannot be avoided in the analysis of each party's ability to address this community's most pressing issues.

Issue by Issue: Where the Major Parties Stand Compared with the African American Community

Abortion

Faced with the history of the eugenics movement and its relationship to Planned Parenthood, the nation's largest abortion provider, increasing numbers of African Americans have begun to support the pro-life agenda. The major problem with the Republican Party on this issue is their lack of concern for the children they save after they are born. The constant perception that they desire to balance budgets on the backs of the poor wins them few friends in minority communities. While Democrats may be out of step with the community on the abortion issue, Republicans have failed to clothe this conversation in the compassion and holistic concern necessary to gain minority support. For this reason African Americans continue to support the pro-choice Democrat agenda even though many recognize abortion's negative impact on an already suffering population.

Death Penalty

This is an area in which the two major parties offer little choice. Both major parties are consistent supporters of the use of capital punishment in order to appear tough on crime. Yet because of the fact that African American males make up a disproportionate percentage of those incarcerated, there is a strong lack of trust in the

American judicial system. With America locking up and executing more people than any other nation in the industrialized world, an alternative criminal justice policy must be provided by one of the parties. African Americans are disproportionately both victims and perpetrators of capital crimes. They also are impacted heavily by the wrongful convictions issue as seen by the recent exonerations of African American death row inmates across the nation. For this reason, there is heavy support for anti-death penalty measures and comprehensive approaches to criminal justice. However, the Democratic Party tends to be as pro-capital punishment as the Republicans. Both Bill Clinton and Barack Obama have been as committed to the continuance of this policy as was George W. Bush. This simple policy commitment has the potential to win countless new supporters.

Welfare

On this issue, the African American community is increasingly divided. Long painted as a group content with life on the public dole, there is an increasingly conservative strand that sees welfare as destructive. While the Democrats extol government programs as the solution to our greatest problems, and the Republicans blast welfare as the destruction of our society, African Americans heavily embrace the centrist view on this issue. Many have seen the damage caused by having generations of families trapped in the cycle of welfare and policy. They are often very frustrated and angered by this occurrence. However, they don't necessarily see cold-hearted policies designed to rip government support from struggling people as the solution. Compassionate and self-empowering programs that represent a mixture of both major political ideologies are supported in large numbers by the African American community. Both parties would be wise to recognize this fact.

School Choice

Because of their heavy involvement with teachers' unions, Democrats are staunchly opposed to the option of school choice in the form of vouchers and charter schools. Yet, often in our communities, desperate parents are willing to embrace any options that will potentially rescue their children. Former Illinois State Senator James Meeks, who also serves as the pastor for Salem Baptist Church in Chicago, has been a strong voucher supporter to the chagrin of his own political party. His efforts to bring this sorely needed reform to public education were overwhelmingly rejected by the Democratic establishment. This is true of many other leaders in the African American community, including Dr. Howard Fuller, founder of the Black Alliance for Education Options. They consistently face opposition from African American political leadership on the issue of school vouchers. Yet polls have shown that minority parents overwhelmingly desire this reform. School choice is a clear area in which the right message could bring significant support from African Americans.

Gun Control

While collective trends reflect uniformity in this area, America's persistent gun violence problem has encouraged increasing division. African Americans are relatively split on this issue. The pro-gun-rights strand of our community has gotten involved in the public debate and rejects the idea that gun ownership is solely for those in rural America. Support in urban America for the recent Supreme Court cases, striking down Chicago's and Washington DC's handgun bans, is clear evidence of this. However, polls have also shown that African Americans traditionally support high levels of gun control. While the pro-gun-ownership contingency may be growing, it still represents the minority opinion. Moderate candidates who support sensible gun control measures will continue to do well among African Americans.

Marriage and Family

California's Proposition 8, defining marriage as a union between one man and one woman, would not have passed without the support of the African American community. On this issue, African American loyalty to the Democrats is especially perplexing. While the overwhelming majority of this community embraces faith and rejects the idea of same-sex marriage, it consistently votes primarily for the party that supports it. Yet support may be weakening as specifically the African American church has been strongly at odds with the Democrats on this issue. President Obama's change in position has also proven to weaken zeal among his most ardent African American supporters. This issue is one that will heavily determine the relationship between African Americans and the Democratic Party in the near future.

Given the aforementioned ideological diversity, the voting patterns of African Americans should reflect a certain heterogeneity. Yet, consistently, this community rewards the Democrats with over 90 percent of the vote. And while the election of Barack Obama to the presidency represents tremendous progress, it may guarantee that African Americans will be in the pocket of the Democratic Party for generations to come. What does this do to a group's political voice? It has the same impact as any monopoly in a free-market economy. The lack of competition for our votes promises that we will constantly have a political party that is unresponsive to our needs. Our continued progress and development requires that we challenge both parties to compete for support. Public policy matters and solutions for the predicament in which African Americans find themselves have no party affiliation. Democrats and Republicans both have strengths and liabilities. The ideological makeup of the African American community reflects an understanding of the systematic causes of poverty coupled with a respect for faith, family, and personal responsibility. For this reason, a significant opportunity exists for reshaping future African American political engagement.

African Americans must embrace a new political agenda that reflects the best of both parties. The faith tradition of this community should heavily influence the development of this agenda. It must include diametrically opposed ideological positions like school choice and investment in public education. It must include government incentives for companies to move to blighted areas, while supporting local entrepreneurship. It must reject the prison industrial complex and the warehousing of millions of Americans while remaining committed to punishing and reforming those whose behavior makes our communities unsafe. It must reform welfare programs that leave many dependent for generations, while exhibiting deep compassion and support for those failing to compete in our current capitalist climate. It must address institutional disparities through programs like affirmative action, while supporting and empowering individuals to overcome these barriers. It must reflect a sense of empathy for the current circumstances in which millions live while pointing a light towards the promise of a greater future. There are no simple answers and the faith community represents the right combination of ideological values and commitments to direct these efforts.

Churches are already taking the lead in many ways. Faith-based local initiatives in areas like prison reform, character development, and violence reduction are areas in which churches can continue to partner with government agencies in addressing some of the most difficult dilemmas. Organizations like Chuck Colsen's Prison Fellowship and Chicago-based Developing Communities Project (DCP) have provided examples of the effectiveness of these efforts. Colson's Prison Fellowship, a faith-based prisoner reform effort, has successfully reduced recidivism rates through its work in 288 prisons across the nation. Working to transform the hearts of America's prison population—the largest in the world—their Christian message has done what the government has been ineffective in doing alone thus far. They have helped to reverse the trend of heavy recidivism in urban communities, thereby altering their political and social conditions.

DCP is a faith-based community organization whose first executive director was Barack Obama. They have shaped the political agenda on Chicago's far South Side around transportation, environmental equality, and education. Furthermore, they have secured both funding and legislative victories in extending transportation service to blighted communities, banning landfills in the area, and reducing rates of drug use through prevention programs. Because their work is primarily in the community in which I live, I have had the great privilege of working with DCP and seeing their efforts firsthand. Their work and organizations like them across the nation are the critical component to developing a holistic and faith-based national plan to transform the conditions of suffering communities.

Once again, the importance of these political solutions is too great to be owned by either political party. Bipartisanship and independence are necessary. Political independence is powerful, and consequently must represent the direction of the future. Until both parties are forced to be responsive to the African American vote, the community will remain in its current quagmire. According to former U.S. Senator, Speaker of the House, and Secretary of State Henry Clay, in politics "there are no permanent friends or no permanent enemies, only permanent interests." Political participation can never serve as a panacea for the problems facing African Americans. Yet if it is used in a way that reflects faith-based principles, and that promotes serious inquiry, ideological diversity, and independence, it can be a powerful tool for social elevation.

6

Countering a Culture of Violence

> *Peace cannot be built on exclusivism, absolutism, and intolerance. But neither can it be built on vague liberal slogans and pious programs gestated in the smoke of confabulation. There can be no peace on earth without the kind of inner change that brings man back to his "right mind."*
>
> —Thomas Merton[1]

Hadiya Pendelton, the honors student murdered blocks from the home of President Obama, is buried nine blocks to the west of my home on the South Side of Chicago. I drive past her gravesite almost every single day. Approximately nine blocks to the north of my home is the monument to murdered teenagers erected by CNN hero Diane Latiker and her organization Kids off the Block. Recently, CNN broadcasted live from this monument in light of the President's visit to Chicago to discuss the issue of gun violence in the nation. I have close friends and students whose lives have been unalterably shattered by this epidemic. The conversation about gun violence is personal. My community represents ground zero of this issue nationally; consequently, I am

---

1. Merton, *Gandi on Non-Violence*, 31.

increasingly frustrated by the partisan and myopic rhetoric I hear surrounding solutions to this problem by our national leaders.

Precipitated by the mass shooting at Sandy Hook Elementary, President Obama and Democratic leaders have moved to ban assault rifles, close the gun show loophole and push for universal background checks for all gun purchases. I respect these efforts as steps in addressing this crisis. However, it is extremely disappointing to know that even if this entire agenda were passed tomorrow, it would do little to address the crisis we face in cities like Chicago.

According to FBI data, there were 12,664 murders in the United States in 2011 alone. Of these, 6,220 cases used handguns, 323 used rifles of some sort, including assault rifles, and 356 used shotguns.[2] If we also consider the 19,000+ suicides by firearms (69 percent by handguns), we must acknowledge that assault rifles are not our nation's most significant problem. Even if we eliminated assault rifles completely, America would still have a very serious problem on its hands.[3]

The rarely discussed truth surrounding the issue of gun violence in the United States is that both the left and the right make valid points in their assessments. The left is correct in recognizing that easy access to high powered guns makes it extremely likely that those guns will be used by people desiring to inflict harm on others. Evidence has proven this time and time again.

While stricter sentencing can help (Chicago's police chief recently stated that under New York State's gun laws Hadiya Pendleton's killer would have been serving a three-year minimum sentence for gun possession and would have never been free to take her life), the right's assumption that legally purchased guns do not contribute to this problem is false. Since 2000, more than half of the guns seized by police in Chicago came from other states. A recent University of Chicago study showed that over 1,300 guns confiscated by police since 2008 were purchased at one Indiana store.[4] Thousands of legally purchased guns from other areas land on the

---

2. Federal Bureau of Investigation, "Murder Circumstances by Weapon."
3. Wintemute et al., "Choice of Weapons."
4. Davey, "Strict Gun Laws."

streets of Chicago each year and contribute to the city's widespread crime. Additionally, the false dichotomy between the "good guys" and the "bad guys" in the world represents an ill-informed and elementary understanding of the moral complexities of human beings. Sometimes those who we assume to be responsible and law-abiding have moral lapses with fatal consequences as well. However, the right is correct in recognizing the fact that creating a new gun law every time the nation has its collective conscience pricked by some heart-wrenching murder or group of murders does little to change the culture of violence faced by our nation. These measures, while politically customary, are the equivalent of putting a band-aid on a gun-shot wound.

Gun violence cannot be simply fixed by a few gun laws but instead requires holistic solutions. A poor economy, a decimated moral climate, the weakened family structure, and poor access to education and mental health services all play a role in producing crime. It is no accident that a recent *Forbes* study showing the ten most violent cities in America reflected cities in which this horrible cocktail of social problems is present.[5] When a political group's response to the tragedies we've faced only involves guns, their overly simplistic and patronizing solutions insult the public's intelligence and bring into question their true commitment to solving this dilemma.

Urban communities are desperate for holistic and sustained approaches to the issue of violence. Violence is clearly not an isolated social phenomenon. In many ways, it is merely a symptom of various other societal ills. Once again, the church community, with its focus on peace, forgiveness, and the collective over the individual, can play a unique role in combating violence. Violence is ultimately a matter of the heart and individual self-control. While addressing the larger problems that foster an environment of violence is important, it cannot replace addressing the spiritual component as well. I recently heard a faith-based anti-violence song by the Grammy-winning rapper Lecrae in which he speaks to young inner-city men. He says, "you are too scared of being broke to think about being better . . . you can forgive much if you understand

---

5. Fisher, "Detroit Tops the 2012 List."

you're forgiven."[6] In this song, he challenges young men to a level of personal change through the theology of sin and forgiveness. He speaks to their hearts in a way that the government cannot. He calls them to transcend their economically insecure circumstances and the depravation of their neighborhoods to reach a place of principled and righteous conduct. His message is that despite the circumstances and the odds stacked against them, they can live on a higher plane. They can be better. A full understanding of their identity in relationship to Christ permits them to not succumb to the deviant behavior that surrounds them. The Christian message of peace, internal transformation, and forgiveness distinctively has the power to transform the lives of those most likely to participate in violent behavior. For this reason, this message and the work of the church are vital.

A plethora of studies have shown faith and church participation to have a positive impact on vulnerable inner-city adolescents. One longitudinal study of 1,725 inner-city youth found that "church attendance tends to buffer the effects of neighborhood disorder on serious crime among black youth: that is, the linkage between a disordered neighborhood and serious crime is not as great when black youth are actively involved in the church."[7] UCLA's James Q. Wilson, through his body of research, has repeatedly asserted that "religion, independent of social class, reduces deviance."[8] "Regular church attendance turns out to be a better predictor than family structure or income, according to a study by Harvard economist Richard Freeman."[9] Even outside of the empirical evidence, intuitively this connection is apparent. Around the nation, local churches are involved in tutoring, conferences, rites of passages, essay and rhetorical contests, concerts, college tours, childcare, health education, and employment preparation for those most susceptible to being perpetrators and victims of violence. Through this work, millions mired in hopelessness have found hope, direction, and a

---

6. LeCrae, "Violence," *Gravity* (Reach Records, 2012).
7. Larson and Johnson, "Religion: The Forgotten Factor."
8. Wilson, "Two Nations."
9. Shapiro and Wright, "Can Churches Save America?" The study referred to is Freeman and Holzer, *Black Youth Employment Crisis*.

social network that reinforces principles essential to their future success. In areas where schools and other institutions fail, churches are "leveraging 10 times their own weight and solving social problems for us," according to Brookings Institution political scientist John DiIulio.[10] The faith community is having a significant impact in America's most troubled areas. Government partnerships that further empower its work, like what has been done through the White House Office of Faith-Based Initiatives, must be supported. Without this vital contribution to the nation, it is clear that our most challenged communities would face even more deplorable conditions.

I have been inspired by a number of faith-based groups that have partnered with local communities in anti-violence efforts. In Philadelphia a group of church members at the Norristown Church began a campaign to walk the streets in violent neighborhoods every Friday and Saturday night during the summer months. Their efforts were aimed at recruiting young men away from criminal behavior and attempting to make their presence felt in a community where violence is rampant. In Boston, a faith-based organization called the Ten Point Coalition was founded to direct inner-city anti-violence efforts on a national scale.[11] Led by the Reverend Eugene Rivers, this partnership with the local police garnered national attention for its unconventional methods used to fight crime. The Philadelphia effort, as well as a number of initiatives in various cities, was born out of this work. In Chicago, ministers like Father Michael Pfleger of St. Sabina' Parish are at the forefront of this mission. He hosts a series of basketball gangs for gang members with the intention of generating conversations and fostering a place of peace. Another Chicago minister, Bill Tomes, was featured in a *Time* magazine article entitled "In the Line of Fire" for repeatedly walking into gang gun fire in order to share the gospel of Christ. In 2010 a group of churches coalesced in Northeastern Detroit to organize a similar movement. Partnering with other community groups, they built a citizen campaign of crime reporting and citizen arrests that contributed to a 15-percent drop in crime from 2009

---

10. Shapiro and Wright, "Can Churches Save America?"
11. Holmes, "Norristown Church Members."

to 2010. While often small in numbers and underfunded, most of these groups have shown the kind of grassroots organization and courage that is necessary to turn the tide in urban America. Lastly, over the past few years I have had the opportunity to participate in a number of church-based rites of passage and sexual purity ceremonies. Done in predominately African American churches, I have seen hundreds of young people launched into adulthood with the encouragement, protection, and support of the faith community. Because this work promotes the values of fidelity, peace, and responsibility it has proven invaluable in countering the culture of inner-city violence.

While the aforementioned represent small examples of the kind of work being done in the faith community, there are thousands of other churches and faith-based non-profits who have organized rallies, marches, mentorship programs, community prayer, job fairs, scholarships, and charity drives in the most at-risk areas in our nation. Their work has the power to break through the political partisanship surrounding gun rights and provide real prospects for social change on the front lines of the nation's most violent communities. Their work is unique and it is important.

Changing the current climate will require a seriously nonpartisan and thoughtful exploration of the true causes of crime. It will equally offend both sides of the aisle and call for equal concessions on deeply held political positions. There will be no change in this nation without it. While I am disappointed in the tepid national policy solutions being pushed, I am heartened that a conversation is occurring. Tragic recent examples of gun violence have at least generated a sense of urgency around this issue. If we miss the opportunity to do something significant now, I fear that the violence we see so frequently will plague future generations in even greater ways. My prayers are that our nation can exhibit a level of political and intellectual maturity that will produce long-term solutions and benefits for generations to come. Our children are counting on us.

7

Marriage and Family Policy

A Foundation for the Future

> *The family is the corner stone of our society. More than any other force it shapes the attitude, the hopes, the ambitions, and the values of the child. And when the family collapses it is the children that are usually damaged. When it happens on a massive scale the community itself is crippled. So, unless we work to strengthen the family, to create conditions under which most parents will stay together, all the rest-schools, playgrounds, and public assistance, and private concern-will never be enough.*
>
> —President Lyndon Johnson[1]

Neither American political party has taken seriously the destruction of this bedrock institution. If one were to listen to political pundits and the mainstream media, they would be convinced that the greatest threats to the American way of life are a rise in gas prices, suicide bombers, and a market that is recovering from a mortgage crisis. Yet the family, as Lyndon Johnson said, is the cornerstone of our society. It doesn't take a rocket scientist

---

1. Johnson, "To Fulfill These Rights." Emphasis added.

Marriage and Family Policy

to realize that all of our efforts to affect change are contingent upon the success or failure of this entity. The United States has the world's highest divorce rate, at slightly over 50 percent. Close to 40 percent of all American children are born out of wedlock and close to 70 percent of all African American children grow up without a father. Poverty rates are drastically higher in single-parent families than in two-parent families, and 70 percent of children in juvenile detention centers come from fatherless homes. This crisis has serious economic implications. When comparing all racial and ethnic groups, poverty rates are identical (6 percent) in two-parent families.[2] This truth receives little attention in our current political wars over the funding of government programs, but its significance is so great that it bears repeating. When families remain intact, poverty is low among all groups, regardless of ethnicity. Furthermore, consider this telling fact: after all of the educational research and innovation, after all of the dollars spent on technology and accountability, the number one factor determining the academic success of a student still is the same as it was two hundred years ago—parental influence. Teachers, administrative innovation, and money spent on technology are all secondary to the substantial role that parents play in education.

Given this trenchant reality, one would think that the unrivaled resources and energy of the American government would be channeled to strengthen the families. Candidate Obama pledged to expand the child care tax credit, support flexible work scheduling initiatives, and expand the Family and Medical Leave Act (FMLA), which provides for paid leave in order to meet a variety of family obligations. While his plan acknowledged the social importance of the family unit, it fell short of the kind of visionary and comprehensive action necessary for the crisis we currently face. Consequently, President Obama, while acknowledging the problem, must go further in efforts to combat it. Even with the FMLA provisions, 40 percent of Americans are not covered and cannot afford to take unpaid leave. Additionally, the United States remains one of only four nations in the world that fails to provide paid maternity

---

2. U.S. Department of Health and Human Services, "Annual Update."

leave. We need bold leadership that will push marriage-and-family-centered curricula in the public schools, continue and expand the marriage and parenting initiatives under the Department of Health and Human Services, challenge the media, which increasingly portrays marriage in a bad light, expand family leave provisions, and strongly fight against efforts to redefine marriage in our society.

The Puritans understood something we do not today. This nation must fully embrace the role of supporting families in the fulfillment of their critical social responsibilities. In fact, the Puritans expressed such great concern that men could lose their families for infractions such as not attending public worship, wild and sinful living, and dereliction in fulfilling parental educational responsibilities. Their vision for a prosperous and peaceful society relied heavily on the moral and civic socialization that could only occur through the structure of the family. Cotton Mather, an influential Puritan minister and political figure, stated in 1679 that "most of the evils that abound amongst us proceed from defects as to family government."[3] He believed that with weak families every social ill known to humankind would be exacerbated. Unfortunately, his predictions have clearly come to fruition today. The Obama Administration has a tremendous opportunity to stem this tide, by turning the nation's attention to the family unit with the same intensity as was seen in the New Deal or the War on Poverty. Anything short of this kind of gargantuan effort will leave this nation with a glaring crack in its foundation. Unfortunately, as any architect will acknowledge, with a crack in the foundation it is only a matter of time before the entire building crumbles.

The good news is that, even in the midst of our current crisis, a number of programs have proven effective in encouraging/restoring African American marriages. In 2001, Nisa I. Muhammad, a Philadelphia resident, took up this call to stem the anti-marriage tide by creating a foundation that sponsors Black Marriage Day in March each year. Since this time, this event, whose goal is to celebrate, strengthen, and encourage marriage, has reached millions. They sponsor courses, discussions, films, and community events

---

3. Morgan, *Puritan Family*, 149.

designed to strengthen the family unit. Consequently, this community-based initiative and others like it are critical to fighting this battle. Furthermore, the faith community has and must continue to play a major role in accomplishing this task. Organizations like the National Black Church Initiative, a coalition of 34,000 churches, have tackled this issue through a nationwide educational effort in support of the family. Furthermore, local churches around the nation are often the chief providers of inner-city-based marriage and parenting programs. Each year there are thousands of marriage classes, seminars, and conferences targeted for African American couples through the church. There is no other institution within these communities that has come close to these efforts. Moreover, consider this fact: "Churchgoing African American women are seventy-three percent more likely to be married at the birth of their child."[4] The church may represent the last bastion of hope for the African American family. Without its influence, the marriage crisis would be substantially worse.

Additionally, the Obama administration has expanded FMLA for military families, extended the Child Tax Credit to cover an additional ten million children, and has provided billions of dollars to help relieve the financial stresses of families through nutrition assistance, childcare, and job training. These efforts are important. However, the shift in focus from marriage-centered programs under President Bush to father-centered programs under President Obama has spread the $100 million a year focused specifically on marriage to general programs of fatherhood and job training. Many marriage-centered organizations, like the California Healthy Marriages Coalition, saw their funding reduced significantly under this philosophical shift. The Obama administration has also taken great steps towards defining marriage as a civil right for homosexual couples. While I choose to refrain from the kind of gay bashing so common in American politics, this cultural shift and its potential impact on an already weak family unit greatly concern me. Consequently, while there are areas in which family policy has been promoted, the aforementioned moves have done a great deal to weaken

---

4. Wilcox and Wolfinger, "Religion and Marriage."

the two parent family structure in our culture. We must encourage and draw attention to what is working in the current administration while challenging it to rethink both its actions and priorities.

I recently asked a group of students to name the most important institution in the African American community. While our previous class discussions had centered on the role of education, the government, and businesses in changing the community, the students unanimously decided that the family was the most critical institution. Second only to this was the church, primarily because of its role in promoting the family. In fact the other institutions were then valued based directly on their ability to support the family. A class of community college students on the South Side of Chicago realized what our greatest scholars and political leaders obviously have not. While we spend countless hours and dollars attempting to build institutions like schools, businesses, and social services in our communities, we spend minimal resources in efforts to bolster the family. Supporting this institution legislatively, socially, and culturally must be central to the national agenda for social change.

While there are a myriad of factors that have caused the decimation of the African American family, a revolution of values is needed to fully counter this phenomenon. The frightening and often-quoted fact that 70 percent of African American children will grow up in a single-parent homes is one that cannot be overemphasized. Sociologist Andrew J. Cherlin of John Hopkins University says African Americans were more likely to be raised by both parents during slavery than today.

There are a multitude of explanations for this phenomenon. They include a history of slavery and discrimination, the war on drugs, welfare policies, the sexual revolution, and a shift in marriage and divorce laws in the nation.

Slavery

While many dismiss its impact, the history of slavery and discrimination cannot be ignored.

Marriage and Family Policy

Lewis Clarke, a former slave who published his experiences in his work *Narrative of the Sufferings of Lewis Clarke*, stated, "I never knew a whole family to live together, till all were grown up, in my life . . ."[5] In twenty-five years of slavery in Kentucky, Clarke was exposed to families who had been torn apart from being sold. His experiences are telling as they represent the significant devastation caused by the evil of slavery. Additionally, in Henry Clary Bruce's book *The New Man: Twenty-Nine Years a Slave*, he further describes this all too common situation.

> My parents belonged to Lemuel Bruce, who died about the year 1836, leaving two children, William Bruce and Rebecca Bruce, who went to live with their aunt, Mrs. Prudence Perkinson; he also left two families of slaves, and they were divided between his two children; my mother's family fell to Miss Rebecca, and the other family, the head of which was known as Bristo, was left to William B. Bruce. Then it was that family ties were broken, the slaves were all hired out, my mother to one man and my father to another. I was too young then to know anything about it, and have to rely entirely on what I have heard my mother and others older than myself say.

For most families, it was unheard of to remain intact for any considerable amount of time.

A study of slave records by the Freedmen's Bureau of 2,888 slave marriages in Mississippi (1,225), Tennessee (1,123) and Louisiana (540), revealed that over 32 percent of marriages were dissolved by masters as a result of slaves being sold away from the family home.[6]

For those who stayed married, rape of the wives was extremely common.

As John Anderson explained: "I did not want to marry a girl belonging to my own place, because I knew I could not bear to see her ill-treated."[7] Moses Grandy agreed he wrote: "no colored man

---

5. Clarke, *Narrative of the Sufferings*, 70.
6. Simkin, "Freeman's Bureau."
7. Simkin, "John Anderson."

wishes to live at the house where his wife lives, for he has to endure the continual misery of seeing her flogged and abused without daring to say a word in her defence."[8] As Henry Bibb pointed out: "If my wife must be exposed to the insults and licentious passions of wicked slave-drivers and overseers, heaven forbid that I should be compelled to witness the sight."[9]

How can marriage and family not be horribly decimated as a result of this environment? How can we now ignore the lingering impact of this culture that just ended legally 150 years ago?

Furthermore, consider that between 1876 and 1965 Jim Crow laws mandated de jure racial segregation that crippled the African American family's ability to participate in many important aspects of American life. During this period married couples had little access to the property rights, criminal justice protections, and security in employment that contribute to stable families. De facto segregation in housing, education, and employment continues. Years of sustained discriminatory public policies are responsible for the current conditions of communities of color. This fact cannot be denied, and any oversimplification ignores the role history plays in shaping the conditions of any group of people. African Americans have experienced 150 years of freedom in this country, with some level of guaranteed protections for these freedoms truly occurring just 50 years ago through the Civil Rights Movement.

The systematic legal, familial, and economic oppression supported through public policy will take generations of targeted counter policies to rectify.

Welfare Policies

Welfare policies of the 1960s and 70s, though well intended, represent another pernicious attack on the African American family. Their impact can be plainly seen today.

It has been clearly documented that the well-intentioned War on Poverty policies that led to changes in the 1960s welfare law had

8. Simkin, "Moses Grandy."
9. Simkin, "Henry Bibb."

Marriage and Family Policy

a deleterious impact on the same group that they were presumably attempting to help. Why? Federal welfare policies mandated that if a woman had a man living in the home they were no longer eligible to receive benefits. This phenomenon is highlighted in the film *Claudine*. Like the main character in this film, many poor women were pressured to choose between the male husband or father figure living in their homes and the receipt of their much-needed benefits. While, ostensibly, it makes sense that the government would preclude women with assumed male financial support from receiving benefits, the impact of this policy was the direct erosion of the family unit. In the early 1960s, the percentage of African American children born to unwed mothers was less than a quarter.[10] Today that number has skyrocketed to 69 percent, with no real end in sight.[11]

Senator Daniel Patrick Moynihan was the first national political figure to connect poverty and welfare policy to the decimation of the family unit. In his 1965 Moynihan Report he warned, "At the heart of the deterioration of the fabric of Negro society is the deterioration of the Negro family. It is the fundamental source of the weakness of the Negro community at the present time." He recognized the destructive impact of policies designed to undermine the family and recommended immediate national action on this critical issue. "In a word, a national effort towards the problems of Negro Americans must be directed towards the question of family structure. The object should be to strengthen the Negro family so as to enable it to raise and support its members as do other families. After that, how this group of Americans chooses to run its affairs, take advantage of its opportunities, or fail to do so, is none of the nation's business."[12] Even though the family crisis had not reached today's levels, he understood what ultimately would happen. If welfare policies continued to provide disincentives for family preservation, the nation would never overcome what he called "its most dangerous social problem." The beauty of Moynihan's Report is that

---

10. Rector, "Reducing Poverty by Revitalizing Marriage."
11. Besharov and West, "African American Marriage Patterns," 99.
12. U.S. Department of Labor, Negro Family (Moynihan Report), ch. 5.

he arrives at conclusions that are difficult to pin as purely liberal or conservative. He both discusses the historic inequities caused by slavery and prescribes the two parent family unit as the most viable long-term solution. Americans often oversimplify this complex issue by failing to understand the history of public policy. The government, while not the only reason for the decimation of the American family, has contributed significantly to this development. As a result, it has an obligation to work to counter this trend.

War on Drugs

The 1980s war on drugs was equally devastating. The United States of America has the unenviable distinction of possessing the world's largest prison population. Much of this can be attributed to the war on drugs and the focus on stiffer sentencing in the 1980s and 90s. One unfortunate externality associated with this effort is the large number of minorities that inevitably bore the brunt of these policies. The Anti-Drug Abuse Act of 1986, for example, included far more severe punishment for the distribution of crack cocaine (associated with poor African Americans) than of powder cocaine (associated with wealthier European Americans). In U.S. criminal justice there is a direct correlation between the income and race of the perpetrator and the amount of time received as a punishment for crimes. As author Michelle Alexander articulates in her book *The New Jim Crow*, "There are more African Americans under correctional control today—in prison or jail, on probation or parole—than were enslaved in 1850, a decade before the Civil War began."[13] The reality of more stringent sentencing for drugs, more common in urban communities, left those communities devoid of large numbers of males.

Even once released, "a criminal freed from prison has scarcely more rights, and arguably less respect, than a freed slave or a black person living 'free' in Mississippi at the height of Jim Crow," argues Alexander.[14] While I do not excuse individual criminal choices, the

13. Alexander, *New Jim Crow*, 180.
14. Ibid., 114.

phenomenon of high incarceration is the result of a larger dynamic. When a particular segment of the population bears a disproportionate portion of its criminal justice efforts, every aspect of the remaining community suffers, including the family.

Sexual Revolution

Moreover, we cannot and must not ignore the permissive sexual culture that has contributed to the decimation of the African American family. Once again, postmodernism has not been the friend of this community. The United States experienced a revolution in sexual values in the 1960s that significantly altered the nation's views of its collective mores. Based on feminist notions of sexual liberation and the introduction of the birth control pill, this era changed America's views of the role of sex and its relationship to family and procreation. Much of the nation began to reject the standards of sexual fidelity in favor of a more liberal approach. Consider the following:

"In the 1950s, six in ten women were virgins at marriage and 87 percent of American women believed that it was wrong for a woman to engage in premarital sex, even with 'a man she is going to marry.' By the time girls born during the sexual revolution came of age, the double standard—in practice, if not exactly in the minds of teenage boys—had been obliterated. Only two in ten of them would be virgins at marriage. Teenagers, in particular, shed the old ways. In 1960, half of unmarried nineteen-year-old women had not yet had sex. In the late 1980s, half of all American girls engaged in sexual intercourse by the age of 17."[15] While instances of teen pregnancy, infidelity, and STD contraction proliferated for all Americans during this time, nowhere was this more damaging than in communities that had little more to rely on than the protections afforded by a strong family unit.

Regrettably, the current culture in the African American community is one in which marriage and fidelity is the exception rather than the norm. And while marriage is declining for all

15. Cohen, "How the Sexual Revolution."

demographics, these rates among African Americans are the lowest in the nation. A climate of marriage-free sexual liberalism further exacerbates the problems of out-of-wedlock births and STD contraction that affect communities of color at larger rates than the national average.

Divorce Laws

The 1970s saw the introduction of no-fault divorce laws designed to make marriage dissolution simpler. Coming on the heels of the sexual revolution, this policy initiative further cemented the idea that marriage and family obligations were more about individual desires than a larger social purpose.

Probably the most well-known no-fault divorce law was enacted in the state of California and signed by Governor Ronald Reagan, coming into effect on January 1, 1970. This came as a rejection of the statutory requirements and time needed for couples to obtain a divorce. Many wanted divorces that were easier to obtain and free from legal complexity. Since 1985, no-fault divorce has been available in most of the fifty U.S. states, with the last holdout, New York, passing legislation in 2010.[16] As a result, from 1960 to 1980 the divorce rate more than doubled—from 9.2 divorces per 1,000 married women to 22.6 divorces per 1,000 married women. This meant that while less than 20 percent of couples who married in 1950 ended up divorced, about 50 percent of couples who married in 1970 did. And approximately half of the children born to married parents in the 1970s saw their parents part, compared to only about 11 percent of those born in the 1950s.[17] Once again, this negative trend was experienced more heavily in poor communities.

As articulated by Bradford Wilcox of *National Affairs*, "In the case of divorce, as in so many others, the worst consequences of the social revolution of the 1960s and '70s are now felt disproportionately by the poor and less educated, while the wealthy elites who set

---

16. "Divorce, American-Style."
17. Wilcox, "Evolution of Divorce."

off these transformations in the first place have managed to reclaim somewhat healthier and more stable habits of married life."[18]

Divorce among African American couples is more prevalent than it is among whites or Hispanic couples, according to a U.S. Census study conducted between 2007 and 2011. The study showed that African American divorce rates (11.5 percent) are slightly higher than European American rates (10.8 percent), and much greater than Hispanic and Asian rates (7.8 and 4.9 percent respectively).[19] These numbers fail to tell the full story of divorces in this country, as they exclude those who have remarried. They do, however, convey important trends. The culture of marriage is compromised among African Americans. African Americans have the lowest rates of marriage among the aforementioned groups. African American women (26 percent) and men (32 percent) are marrying at significantly lower rates than European American women (51 percent) and men (44 percent).[20]

Many have theorized that the economic stress of living in poverty puts additional strains on marriage and accounts for this dynamic. However, this is debatable as many poor immigrant communities do not share this trend. What is more important than analyzing the possible reasons is highlighting the fundamental role that marriage plays in stabilizing communities and advocating for its protection at the national level. What many policy leaders continue to ignore is that marriage has irrefutable individual and collective social benefits. The following data only tells a small portion of the story.

- Married couples build more wealth on average than singles or cohabiting couples.

- Married women are at lower risk for domestic violence than women in cohabiting or dating relationships.

- Boys raised in single-parent homes are more likely to engage in criminal and delinquent behavior than those raised by two married biological parents.

18. Ibid.
19. "Selected Social Characteristics."
20. Statistic Brain Research Institute, "Marriage Statistics."

- Married mothers have lower rates of depression than single or cohabiting mothers, probably because they are more likely to receive practical and emotional support from their child's father and his family.
- Children raised in married homes are more likely to stay in school, have fewer behavioral and attendance problems, and earn four-year college degrees.
- Married women are economically better off than divorced, cohabiting, and never-married women.
- Marriage generates social capital. The social bonds created through marriage yield benefits not only for the family but for others as well, including the larger society.[21]

Marriages stabilize communities, protect children, and provide significant social and economic benefits to its participants. They have the ability to mitigate the damage of some of our most perplexing social issues. When strong marriages exist at the core of a society, they lessen the need for government social services. For this reason, America has a vested interest in assuring both their health and preservation.

While I know it is unpopular in our current political climate, I still believe in the wisdom of the world's bestselling book. Before establishing any other social institution, God established the family. He gives this institution a very clear purpose: "Has not the one God made you? You belong to him in body and spirit. And what does the one God seek? Godly offspring" (Mal 2:15 NIV). He also gives them a clear mandate and direction. "Start children off on the way they should go, and even when they are old they will not turn from it" (Prov 22:6 NIV). As simplistic as this direction may sound, it is clear that the front lines of cultural change may not be in the halls of Congress, but in the nation's living rooms. We must stand firm in this reality and demand that our executive leadership enacts true

---

21. See Institute for American Values, "Why Marriage Matters"; California Healthy Marriages Coalition, "Healthy Marriages, Healthy Lives"; National Healthy Marriage Resource Center, "Testimony of Dr. Barbara Dafoe Whitehead."

border security; the kind designed to protect America's families from a culture that increasingly sees their survival as insignificant.

8

Education Reform

The Civil Rights Issue of This Generation

He who opens a school door, closes a prison.

—Victor Hugo[1]

My mother has spent most of her life in education. As college administrator, high school teacher, and educational consultant, she modeled a commitment to education that left an indelible mark on me. Being a first generation college graduate, she faced sometimes insurmountable obstacles to achieve her dream of attaining both undergraduate and graduate level degrees. I witnessed the transformative power of education for not only individuals, but also the communities from which they came. Education may be the most vital tool that exists in this nation for social mobility. College graduates earn $20,000 a year more than high school graduates and close to $500,000 more over their lifetimes. Of America's prison population, the largest in the world, 82 percent are high school dropouts. Those we fail to educate become

1. Online: http://www.brainyquote.com/quotes/quotes/v/victorhugo 104893.html.

part of a permanent underclass. Every dollar invested in a child is one less dollar spent later on criminal justice. For this reason, the current crisis facing the American education system has received significant attention in recent years. Education reform has become one of America's greatest priorities. A recent Organization for Economic Cooperation and Development (OECD) Program for International Student Assessment (PISA) report, which compares the knowledge and skills of fifteen-year-olds in seventy countries around the world, ranked the United States fourteenth out of thirty-four OECD countries for reading skills, seventeenth for science, and twenty-fifth for mathematics.[2] Even more troubling: out of the thirty-four OECD countries, only eight have a lower high school graduation rate than the US. [3]

Yet only three of these nations spend more than we do educating our students. Currently, the United States spends just over $10,000 per pupil per year, compared to $2,307 in 1980 and $842 in 1970. We pour increasing amounts of money into education, yet our schools have remained collectively deficient. In the African American community the seriousness of this crisis is even more acute. African American students consistently score below already sliding national averages and are routinely subjected to inferior and underfunded educational institutions. The tragedy in these statistics is that education still represents America's greatest hope for social mobility.

Since the 1896 Supreme Court ruling *Plessy v. Ferguson*, America's slave descendants have battled for educational parity. While 1954's *Brown v. Board of Education* outlawed Plessy's government-sanctioned segregation, the fifty-plus years that have followed have still failed to provide full educational equality. And with the Supreme Court's 2007 ruling that deemed court ordered integration to be unconstitutional, America's two-tier education system appears to have a strong future. Consider the following statistics:

- In 2005, only 55 percent of all black students graduated from high school on time with a regular diploma, compared

2. Dougherty, "If America Spends More."
3. National Center for Education Statistics, "OECD: Trends."

to 78 percent of whites.[4]

- In 2002, 23 percent of all black students who started public high school left it prepared for college, compared to 40 percent of whites.[5]
- On average, African American and Hispanic twelfth-grade students read at approximately the same level as white eighth-graders.[6]
- Of students who graduated with the class of 2007, African Americans scored lower than all other racial and ethnic groups on all three parts of the SAT.[7]
- In the forty-nine states studied, the school districts with the highest minority enrollments receive an average of $877 less per student than school districts with the lowest number of minorities enrolled.[8]

These grim statistics are trenchant examples of the depth of the crisis that is faced. From the Department of Education to local school boards, America has spent billions of dollars generating solutions. Yet at the heart of their inability to solve this conundrum lies a fundamental ideological flaw. Many assume that the future of education lies solely with the reform of the existing public school system. It does not.

School choice represents the future of education. For this reason, unless the United States adopts true reform that recognizes the importance of both public and private school options, we will remain in our current predicament. In Chicago, graduation rates at public charter high schools are 21 percentage points better than public high schools, and charter school students are twice as likely to go to college. Because voucher and charter schools are started by people within local communities, they inevitably allow these communities to have a heavier level of influence. Take Chicago's

4. Editorial Projects in Education Research Center, *Diplomas Count 2008*.
5. Greene and Winters, "Public High School Graduation."
6. U.S. Department of Education, "High School Reading: Key Issue Brief."
7. College Board, "2007 College-Bound Seniors," Table 8.
8. Education Trust, "Funding Gap."

Urban Prep as an example. This all-African-American-male charter school on Chicago's Southside has sent every one of its graduates to college since its inception. This accomplishment is more noteworthy considering that the community, from which most of these students come, has some of the highest levels of social dysfunction in the entire nation. These are the kinds of successes that can occur when local communities have the freedom to tackle education using unique and innovative methods. Furthermore, private schools, specifically, those with a religious mission, have proven to be effective alternatives to a struggling public school system. In 2007, 5,072,451 students attended 33,740 private elementary and secondary schools. Of these students, 74.5 percent were Caucasian, non-Hispanic, 9.8 percent were African American, 9.6 percent were Hispanic, 5.4 percent were Asian or Pacific Islander, and .6 percent were Native American. The average school size was 150.3 students. There were 456,266 teachers. The number of students per teacher was about eleven. In private schools, 65 percent of seniors went on to attend a four-year college.[9]

What the aforementioned statistics make abundantly clear is this: private schools are able to offer significantly smaller school and class sizes and have a higher rate of four-year college attendance than their public school counterparts. Additionally, while the bulk of minority students (and all students for that matter) attend public schools, those in private schools perform more strongly on average. Private schools represent an opportunity for a variety of students to succeed. For this reason, the academic and economic segregation that locks most minority students into failing public schools must end.

In his book *Beyond Memory and Vision: The Case for Faith-Based Schools*, Dr. Steven Vryhof provides evidence that religious schools are not only effective at winning parental support, but also at meeting national testing standards. Contrary to the myth of inferior academic performance, he proves that because religious schools are able to offer a consistent moral ethos, an overarching and comprehensive vision, and a supportive extended community,

---

9. Birnbaum, "Parents can plumb the Web."

they excel academically. He references the National Educational Longitudinal Study began in 1988 (NELS:88), which states that tests in reading, math, science, and social studies are all higher in private Christian schools. Yet the data also suggests that even students from less socioeconomically advantaged homes achieve at the same high level in these academic settings. This fact is not well known, yet it is significant. He also highlighted Christian schools in a variety of communities that have encouraged parental involvement through contracts, interviews, and clearly defined academic and faith expectations. Subsequently, his data reflects the reality that private school parents volunteer with their schools (60 percent) at much higher rates than their public school counterparts (14 percent). All of this is done while working with significantly lower substantial budgets, which results in teachers being paid approximately half of what public school teachers receive.

President Theodore Roosevelt said that "to educate a man in the mind but not in the morals is to educate a menace to society." Private religious schools have the unique ability to address the holistic development of a child in a way that our segmented secular education system does not.

As a product of a Catholic middle and high school, I benefited greatly from the discipline, culture, and opportunity to wrestle with moral and social issues from a Christian perspective that these schools provided.

This proved invaluable to my spiritual, academic, and intellectual development as a young male.

While the American education system expends a great deal of effort to teach skills like reading and writing, the moral development of our children is often left to chance. Most American students graduate without any serious reflection on their spiritual and intellectual worldview, nor any real attention to the ethical and personal issues that serve as the downfall of many a successful person. Topics like conflict management, marriage, personal temperance, ethical decision making, and many others are either completely ignored or are conveyed from a disconnected and inconsistent perspective that does little for a student's overall development. This holistic approach to education is essential for success. Skill-based education, devoid of an ideological framework that provides a motive behind the use of those skills, does little to elevate our society. Whether one considers oneself religious or not, this reality should be acknowledged by all segments of the public.

Most European countries have approved some form of vouchers to give parents control over their children's education. It has allowed for parents to send their children to the best schools for them, including those that teach values consistent with their religious faith. The United States has failed to follow suit although 60 percent of Americans support school vouchers and charter schools. In both Cleveland and Milwaukee, vouchers have led to more integrated schools. In Milwaukee voucher students graduate at much higher rates than public school students. We must explore new options in education. While no solution is a panacea, school choice may be one of our best hopes.

The connection between education and social mobility cannot be understated. Urban economists and developers look at the failure of schools in their projections about the number of jails that need to be built in the future. By failing to provide equal educational access, we lock a large segment of our nation into a permanent underclass status. For this reason, we cannot afford to leave any corrective options off of the table. People often argue about whether vouchers and charter schools destroy unions or serve to abandon the public school system. Yet these represent false choices. Beyond the political rhetoric lie solutions that adequately address the concerns of a variety of segments of the society. It is possible to both support public schools and provide options for students and parents. They do not represent mutually exclusive goals. And while many also question the constitutionality of voucher programs under the notion of the separation of church and state, these concerns are unfounded. In 2002 the Zellman v. Simmons-Harris Supreme Court decision upheld the Constitutionality of voucher programs declaring that they were essentially neutral towards religion because they provided aid to parents who made independent and private choices. It is foolish to prevent the faith-based community from uniquely addressing the moral and intellectual development of young people in a way that secular schools are ill equipped to do. Our political system should provide it the freedom to do so.

While I agree with President Obama on a variety of issues, this is one with which I take issue. Although he acknowledges the failures of the testing culture created through No Child Left Behind and has made educational reform a priority, he refuses to provide full school choice. His rejection of the DC Opportunity Scholarship, a voucher program that would have sent hundreds of inner-city students to private schools, is indefensible. By catering to the political left he has denied countless low-income students the same opportunities his two daughters have received. I have been fortunate enough to send my own children to a private religious school in Chicago's south suburbs. While this decision represents a serious financial sacrifice, as a parent I am willing to do all I can to ensure a quality education for my children. Parental involvement is still the most significant factor determining the academic success of a child. Beyond teacher quality, school technology, the length of the school day, and a variety of other foci of the reform movement, parents are still paramount. It is simple. Those children who have supportive parents typically do well, and those who do not often fail. Empowering parents is good public policy. All parents, wealthy or poor, want school choice. Yet true school choice only exists in this nation for those with money. This must change.

This policy proposition in no way represents an effort to abandon America's public schools. I refuse to accept the idea that as a nation we cannot create a solution to our education crisis that is fair to both the current public system and parents. In my life I have benefited from both public and parochial institutions. Both play an important role in our society. Americans from all perspectives want education reform. Yet when the federal government commits roughly 3 percent of its budget to education, inequality at the state level is bound to occur. We must fund our schools equally across the board, and devote additional time and attention to strengthening the nation's public schools. However, education is holistic. It is also different for every child. A blind commitment to a secular, inflexible education system is a mistake. When America makes education a real priority, and puts children ahead of ideology, we will no longer have to waste time debating about splitting limited resources between public and private schools. We will both provide equal funding for all students and allow for true diversity in our approach to education.

We can and must provide a healthy and competitive public school system while simultaneously providing educational options for those families for whom the traditional public school setting is less desirable. American children, specifically African American children, do not have time for partisanship with respect to this issue. They must have these options now.

The conversation surrounding education reform must transcend our myopic self-interests and move toward solutions in the best interests of all schools and all communities. None of us can end our concern for education at the point at which our own children are educated. Educational equity is a matter of justice. Public schools are poignant reminders of the economic and social disparities that are so common in the United States. A recent Stanford University study found that the gap in standardized test scores between affluent and low-income students grew by about 40 percent since the 1960s.[10] Another study, conducted by the University of Michigan, found the gap in college completion among rich and poor children has grown by 50 percent in the past twenty-five years.[11] Consequently, even though I support private schools, the greater issue of educational justice in both public and private forms is a cause around which we all can rally.

On this issue as well, the African American faith community is poised to bring a unique contribution. In addition to historically providing educational options for underserved students, they also have been great supporters of local public schools. They are responsible for establishing thousands of elementary, high schools, and colleges across the country in addition to being great supporters of public school families, principals, and teachers in underserved areas. Many understand the Calvinist principle of common grace, suggesting that equitable public schools are within the realm of

---

10. Reardon, "Widening Academic Achievement Gap."
11. Bailey and Dynarski, "Gains and Gaps."

God's concern for humanity. They have proven that it is entirely possible for Christians to simultaneously recognize the importance of vibrant faith-based educational institutions and their secular counterparts. A respect for pluralism and a commitment to the nation's children demands this.

In cities around the nation, the current conversation around educational reform is full of vitriol as teachers, parents, administrators, activists, and political figures fight over a host of issues including accountability, funding, and school closings. Interest groups stake their territory and dig in to unmovable ideological positions. We need a new vision for our schools that recognizes that the various community stakeholders have common interests and that embracing a spirit of cooperation and compromise is the only path to true reform. The faith community, through its history of humbly serving the greater public, extending compassion to the least in our society, and empowering the masses through education, can play an important role in making this reform effective. The Bible reminds us that what we impart to our children will leave an enduring impression on them (Deut 6:7). If we want to live in a society that is prosperous, educated, and civil, we must assure an equitable, competitive, and value-based education for all of our citizens. I look forward to the day that this occurs.

9

Entrepreneurship

The Key to Prosperity

Entrepreneurs and their small enterprises are responsible for almost all the economic growth in the United States.

—Ronald Reagan[1]

I come from a family of entrepreneurs. When I was twelve years old, my father moved our entire family from the south suburbs of Chicago to South Bend, Indiana, for an opportunity he had to pursue a career dream. After completing Ford's dealer training program he was provided an opportunity to own a Lincoln Mercury, Nissan, Saab, Hyundai dealership. After fifteen successful years in this industry, he retired briefly to subsequently pursue a career as a McDonald's franchise owner. In this venture he has found his greatest level of success and continues to build an impressive multi-franchise enterprise.

What I saw in his life and work would leave an indelible impression upon me for the rest of my life. I witnessed firsthand the

---

1. Online: http://www.brainyquote.com/quotes/quotes/r/ronaldreag183751.html.

level of commitment and dedication it took to take an idea and move it to fruition. I saw the truth behind Einstein's quote that "Genius is 1 percent inspiration and 99 percent perspiration."[2] Through his example, he taught both my brother and me that labor and industry were as important as talent and opportunity. He laid an economic foundation that has paid great dividends in our lives as adults. Yet this feat was not easy. My father was well aware of the challenges facing Americans of color. He also faced tremendous obstacles in an environment in which he was often expected to fail. For this reason, he consistently emphasized responsibility, hard work, and entrepreneurship for his sons.

Entrepreneurship is the key to economically uplifting communities of color. It has always been the pulse of the American economy. One area most germane to the goal of social change among African Americans is business ownership. It is no secret that most urban communities around the nation suffer from the same lethal combination of unemployment, crime, poverty, and a lack of business ownership. Small businesses represent the front lines of changing this dynamic. Unfortunately, no amount of outside intervention can replace locally based employment and business ownership. Even when large employers like Wal-Mart come into struggling areas, they ultimately are ineffective at transforming the long-term economic conditions of the majority of residents. This happens because although corporations can provide jobs and a tax base, most of the revenue they gain leaves the local community. Furthermore, they are much less invested than the local entrepreneur, who often has deep ties in the areas in which they serve. As has been evidenced in countless examples around the nation, when a large company makes a decision to leave an area it leaves in its wake thousands of economically devastated communities, families, and individuals. Corporate priorities are primarily connected to larger global financial commitments. For this reason, corporations alone cannot best provide for the long-term economic health of a community. While large corporations do important work and have a significant national economic role to play, neighborhoods flourish

2. Online: http://www.brainyquote.com/quotes/quotes/t/thomasaed109928.html.

Entrepreneurship

when local businesses flourish. They represent the lifeline of any area. When they fail, communities fail.

While often underreported, African Americans have a wealth of business success on which to build. In a 2007 U.S. Census survey, "From 2002 to 2007, the number of black-owned businesses increased by 60.5 percent to 1.9 million, more than triple the national rate of 18.0 percent," and during the same period, "receipts generated by black-owned businesses increased 55.1 percent to $137.5 billion." African Americans were most likely to own businesses in health care and social assistance, and in repair, maintenance, personal, and laundry services sectors. These businesses employed 921,032 people and had payrolls that totaled $23.9 billion.[3] This reflects a significant amount of promise and opportunity for entrepreneurship within urban communities. Cities like New York, Chicago, Houston, and Detroit, which possess the largest number of these enterprises, are also areas whose social conditions can most benefit from their growth and expansion. There is much on which to build.

However, this situation is more complicated. While the aforementioned numbers are promising, they do not tell the complete story. According to economist Robert Fairlie of the University of California Santa Cruz, "Only 3.8 percent of blacks own their own business, compared with 6 percent of Latinos and 11.6 percent of whites and Asian Americans. Business failure rates during the first four years are 27 percent for black-owned firms compared with 22.5 percent for white-owned businesses. Only 14 percent of black-owned businesses generate annual profits of $10,000 or more, compared with 30 percent of white-owned firms, and black businesses are less likely to employ others (11 percent compared with 21 percent)."[4]

The condition of African American entrepreneurship, while promising, still reflects an inability to compete with much of the rest of the nation. Clearly, the subsequent higher rates of unemployment, crime, and incarceration are a direct consequence. In order

---

3. U.S. Census Bureau, "Census Bureau Reports."
4. McNulty, "Economists deciphers racial disparities."

The Way Out

to empower this segment of our nation to fully claim the American dream, we must address this disparity. No realistic efforts to elevate communities of color can occur without a commitment to business development. And unfortunately, most African Americans have only seen the current state of economic devastation today and are unaware of models of success that existed.

Probably the greatest hope for business-based community development can be seen in the town of Tulsa, Oklahoma, in the early 1900s. This area, known as "Black Wall Street," was one of the most affluent communities of color that has ever existed in the United States. The thirty-six-block area boasted myriad businesses, including thirty grocery stores, twenty-one restaurants, twenty-one churches, two movie theaters, pawn shops, brothels, jewelry stores, a hospital, a bank, a post office, libraries, schools, law offices, half dozen private airplanes, and even a bus system. The dollar circulated thirty-six to one hundred times among this local population. There was a solid infrastructure and self-contained economic system that generated a substantial amount of wealth for the thousands of residents of the community. Unfortunately this prosperity did not last. On June 1, 1921, race riots broke out and within a period of twelve hours most of this community was destroyed. Ku Klux Klan members from neighboring communities attacked the area and commenced hours of gunfights and massive bloodshed. There are even accounts of incendiary bombs dropped from military airplanes on the area during this one-day period.[5] Three thousand African Americans were left dead at the end of the carnage and most of the community's businesses were lost.[6]

While many choose to focus on the tragedy in this sad event, what strikes me are the trenchant possibilities that lie in this example. There is great hope in communities like that of Tulsa in the early 1900s. Entrepreneurship, small business ownership, and economic policies that support local economies are good for all of the United States. National legislation like NAFTA has had a deleterious impact on local economies in all of America, including communities

---

5. Madigan, *Burning: Massacre, Destruction*, 4, 131–32, 144, 159, 164, 249.

6. Wilson and Wallace, *Black Wallstreet*.

of color. Though we live and breathe globalization as Americans, we must strive to maintain a level of commitment to local protectionism in order to guarantee our own national economic future.

While there are many studies about this question, most economists agree that approximately 90 percent of the wealth within inner cities is spent in non-African-American businesses. This dynamic assures that these neighborhoods will remain trapped in a vicious cycle of poverty. The billions of dollars spent each year in communities of color, if spent locally, could do infinitely more to uplift people than any amount of social welfare. Neighborhoods in which businesses thrive are neighborhoods that have a reduced need for the various social programs on which so many urban communities depend. The nation's leaders must approach this issue understanding the power of social change through reinforcing entrepreneurship.

Promising legislative efforts like the Urban Enterprise Zone initiative have poured millions of dollars in tax incentives for companies to invest in blighted communities. This legislation, which promotes both small and larger businesses, is the kind of work that must be encouraged, supported, and expanded if urban economic development is going to be taken seriously.

In devastated areas around the nation, this federal initiative has accomplished a great deal in boosting business development since its inception in the mid 1980s. With a simple 3-percent sales tax savings, cities like Elizabeth, New Jersey, have stimulated over $1.5 billion in economic investment.[7] The city of Newark, New Jersey, boasts support for over two thousand local businesses through this program[8] and in Hammond, Indiana, there has been $500 million in private investment and the creation of four thousand new local jobs.[9] While no legislation is a panacea, these kinds of long-term and locally empowering efforts represent the right focus for uplifting the parts of our nation that have been left behind.

---

7. Online: http://www.elizabethnj.org/business/urban-enterprise-zone-uez.

8. Online: http://www.newarkuez.org.

9. Online: http://www.helpinghammond.com/FrontEnd/Home.php.

The Way Out

Solutions to these conundrums are not mutually exclusive. Faith, family, education, and political engagement are all important. However, in a capitalist system, money is power.

Economic development can and should be promoted by both the business and faith community alike. With respect to this topic, I reject the notion that faith and economic principles are separate. The Bible lays out a myriad of important principles that lead to fiscal responsibility and prosperity. In fact, the American capitalist notion of the "Puritan work ethic" comes from the Puritans' commitment to hard work and self-sacrifice. Without their influence and biblically inspired example, it is difficult to argue that capitalism in this country could have developed in the way it has. The Scriptures remind us that "*All hard work* brings a profit, but mere talk leads only to poverty" (Prov 14:23, NIV). While this formula does not account for the legal and social injustices fixed deeply in the history of American capitalism, coupled with responsible government policy, it does provide the best hope for the future progress of disadvantaged Americans. As previously mentioned, churches around the nation are on the front lines of fostering economic development in blighted areas. They run credit unions, support local businesses, and train citizens on the principles of financial management and entrepreneurship. Pastor Bill Winston's Living Word Ministries on Chicago's Westside has a business incubator and entrepreneurship training center that trains hundreds of people each year to start businesses in poor communities. They represent one illustration among thousands of churches around the nation fighting to secure the economic future of urban America. Their work must be supported by all sectors of society, including the government, as it is crucial. The challenges are enormous and there is so much more to be done.

The diligent spirit at the heart of entrepreneurship lies deeply in the African American community. Fostering this spirit is essential to rescuing millions from the quagmire of poverty and despair. The problems facing communities of color are neither to be blamed solely on the government nor the individual. They are much more complex. Real solutions must take into account both realities. We must encourage an environment in which local businesses can

Entrepreneurship

thrive through individual initiative and the wise stewardship of resources. There exists a tremendous amount of individual economic potential in all parts of this nation. It must be harnessed. This, however, does not negate the government's responsibility for fostering this environment. Separating this conversation from the government's historic role in promoting economic inequality is both foolish and myopic. We must recognize the equal function of the government, the individual, and the business community in advancing this important economic agenda. A balanced and reasoned understanding of this nation's problems with class and inequality mandates this approach.

10

Personal Reflections

Yesterday is gone. Tomorrow has not yet come. We have only today. Let us begin.

—Mother Teresa[1]

The challenges facing our nation and communities of color are daunting. As I write this, I am well aware that we face persistent rates of poverty, fatherlessness, educational failure, and crime. Yet I am also aware that hope does exist. One of the most inspirational films I have seen in recent years is a football film produced by a church in Georgia called *Facing the Giants*. It is the story of a losing team that has given in to an attitude of defeat, depression, and despair as a consequence of their consistent failures on the field. As typical in a football film, one coach turns the team around and calls them to be champions. What is astounding about this film is that the team never changes coaches. The losing coach learns to win and his major inspiration is faith in God. As he fights to restore his own faith, he pushes his players to the same victory,

---

1. Online: http://www.goodreads.com/quotes/44552-yesterday-is-gone-tomorrow-has-not-yet-come-we-have.

first internally, then externally. The result is great success on the field and in his personal life.

As many people, I have looked at the crisis in the African American community and have struggled at times to have hope. Yet I speak as a product of the principles discussed in this book. My life has been a testimony of the power of faith, family, and personal industry. My immediate and extended family has provided copious examples of professional and personal accomplishment for which I am forever grateful. I come from a family of educators, entrepreneurs, public servants, corporate executives, doctors, lawyers, and civil servants. Most were as devoted to faith and family as they were to their careers. Yet their examples are not the only upon which I have drawn. The family patriarchs and matriarchs who forsook their own ambitions to raise a total of fifteen children between the four of them are ultimately the sole reason any of these successes were possible. Their loyalty to family and community is the base on which our achievement is built. In raising our own children, my wife and I can only hope to replicate much of what we have seen while adding our unique perspectives and values. There are thousands of African American families who share a similar story. In these experiences is a model on which future communities can be built.

I recognize that any situation can change with the right focus. The problem is not that communities of color are hopelessly trapped in despair; the problem is that America has not focused on the right solutions. While government can be a great tool for addressing a variety of conundrums we face, it cannot replace institutions like the family, church, and business communities. Government should be one of the last resorts in solving our problems, not the first. Government's greatest function should be to support, not replace these institutions. While it has the distinctive ability of being society's most well-resourced and organized institution, there is a danger in an overreliance on its influence. Not only does it have the potential to help many, it has the simultaneous ability to oppress, restrict, and stifle their freedom and development as well. Developing long-term solutions to the plethora of challenges facing communities of color requires the government to play a healthy, limited, and community empowering role. Both too much and too little governmental involvement will have equally damaging consequences.

I am not a blind ideologue with respect to the role of government nor the role of the faith community. This work is an effort to transcend conversations of blame and accusation in order to create a space for solutions and progress. I am less interested in issues of collective culpability as I am in remedies. There is enough liability to be shared. Moreover, I am convinced that blind partisanship and sectarianism preclude this nation from solving many of its dilemmas. For this reason, I am equally disinterested in them. As George Washington reminded us, partisanship serves strictly "to put, in the place of the delegated will of the nation the will of a party." No party, denomination, nor ethnic group has the market cornered on the truth with respect to this discussion. We all bring needed contributions critical to moving forward.

The Bible is full of stories of hope. I am reminded of the greatest one of these stories, that of a Savior who was opposed by the establishment of his day and paid the ultimate price for his vision of the world. He had no army, large federal budget, nor political position of influence. Yet he changed the world in just three short years of ministry. His death, ironically, is the greatest symbol of life and hope that the world has known. It is for this reason that I believe in the ability of the African American community to chart a new course. We must build on the past while blazing an ambitious path for the future. It will take us reclaiming the greatest parts of our history while we capitalize on the opportunities that exist in this generation. It will also take a holistic and multi-institutional approach that rejects the myopic nature of current political and cultural conversations. As Dr. King said, "Human progress is neither automatic nor inevitable. . . . Every step toward the goal of justice requires sacrifice, suffering, and struggle; the tireless exertions and passionate concern of dedicated individuals."

It will also take an understanding of our unique place in history and a reclaiming of the faith that has served us so well. This faith has brought us through a level of suffering that few groups in modern history have known. Consequently, I am a firm believer

Personal Reflections

that this faith, coupled with a broad commitment to civic, political, and economic life, represents our best hope for the future.

Our best days are still ahead of us.

Bibliography

Al-Fadhli, Hussain M., and Thomas Michael Kersen. "How Religious, Social, and Cultural Capital Factors Influence Educational Aspirations of African American Adolescents." *The Journal of Negro Education* 79/3 (Summer 2010) 380–89, 438–39.

Alexander, Michelle. *The New Jim Crow: Mass Incarceration in the Age of Colorblindness.* New York: New Press, 2010.

Bailey, Martha J., and Susan M. Dynarski. "Gains and Gaps: Changing Inequality in U.S. College Entry and Completion." NBER Working Paper 17633. Cambridge: National Bureau of Economic Research, 2011.

Barna Group. "Church Attendance." Online: http://www.barna.org/FlexPage.aspx?Page=Topic&TopicID=10.

———. "How the Faith of African Americans Has Changed." https://www.barna.org/culture-articles/286-how-the-faith-of-african-americans-has-changed?q=blacks+african.

———. "Morality Continues to Decay." November 3, 2003. Online: http://www.barna.org/barna-update/article/5-barna-update/129-morality-continues-to-decay.

Barnes, Rebecca, and Lowry, Lindy. "Special Report: The American Church in Crisis." *Outreach Magazine*, May/June 2006. Online: http://simplechurchathome.com/PDF&PowerPoint/AmericanChurchCrisis.pdf.

Besharov, Douglas J., and Andrew West. "African American Marriage Patterns." In *Beyond the Color Line: New Perspectives on Race and Ethnicity in America*, edited by Abigail Thernstrom and Stephan Thernstrom, 95–113. New York: Manhattan Institute; Standford, CA: Hoover Institution Press, 2002. Online: http://media.hoover.org/documents/0817998721_95.pdf.

Birnbaum, Michael. "Parents can plumb the Web for data on private schools." *Washington Post*, November 2, 2009. Online: http://www.washingtonpost.com/wp-dyn/content/article/2009/11/01/AR2009110101878.html.

Bositis, David A. "Blacks and the 2004 Democratic National Convention." Washington, DC: Joint Center for Political and Economic Studies, July 2004. Online: http://www.jointcenter.org/sites/default/files/upload/research/files/2004%20Democratic%20Convention%20Guide.pdf.

Bibliography

Bradley, Anthony. "Inner City Churches Sustain Education Success." *World Magazine*, June 8, 2001. Online: http://www.worldmag.com/2011/06/inner_city_churches_sustain_education_success.

Briggs, David. "Cleveland Churches Take Open Approach to Teen Abstinence Efforts." June 13, 2008. Online: http://blog.cleveland.com/lifestyles/2008/06/cleveland_churches_take_open_a.html.

Brooks, David. "If It Feels Right . . ." *New York Times*, Op-Ed, September 12, 2011. Online: http://www.nytimes.com/2011/09/13/opinion/if-it-feels-right.html.

California Healthy Marriages Coalition. "Healthy Marriages, Healthy Lives: Research on the Alignment of Health, Marital Outcomes and Marriage Education." Online: http://www.camarriage.com/research/index.ashx?nv=8&pg=45.

Carson, Emmett D. *A Hand Up: Black Philanthropy and Self Help in America*. Washington, DC: Joint Center for Political and Economic Studies Press, 1993.

Clarke, John Henrik. "Paul Robeson: The Artist as Activist and Social Thinker." In *Paul Robeson: The Great Forerunner*, editors of Freedomways, 189–201. New York: Dodd, Mead, 1978.

Clarke, Lewis Garrard. *Narrative of the Sufferings of Lewis Clarke, during a Captivity of More Than Twenty-Five Years, among the Algerines of Kentucky, One of the So Called Christian States of North America*. Boston: David H. Ela, 1845.

Clinton, Bill. *My Life*. New York: Vintage, 2004.

Cohen, Nancy L. "How the Sexual Revolution Changed America Forever." AlterNet.org, February 5, 2012. Online: http://www.alternet.org/story/153969/how_the_sexual_revolution_changed_america_forever.

College Board. "2007 College-Bound Seniors: Total Group Profile Report." Online: http://www.collegeboard.com/prod_downloads/about/news_info/cbsenior/yr2007/national-report.pdf.

Cone, James. *Black Theology and Black Power*. Maryknoll, NY: Orbis, 1969.

Davey, Monica. "Strict Gun Laws in Chicago Can't Stem Fatal Shots." *New York Times*, January 30, 2013, A1.

Davis, F. James. *Who Is Black?: One Nation's Definition*. University Park: Pennsylvania State University Press, 1991.

Dictionary.com Unabridged. Random House, Inc., 2013. Online: http://dictionary.reference.com/.

"Divorce, American-Style: No-Fault Is Now the Law in All 50 states." *Consumer Reports*, October 13, 2010. Online: http://news.consumerreports.org/money/2010/10/new-york-legal-no-fault-divorce-law-50-states-.html.

Dougherty, Michael Brendan. "If America Spends More Than Most Countries per Student, Then Why Are Its Schools So Bad?" *Business Insider*, January 7, 2012. Online: http://www.businessinsider.com/us-education-spending-compared-to-the-rest-of-the-developed-world-2012-1.

Bibliography

Douglass, Frederick. "Slaveholding Religion and the Religion of Christ." In Appendix to *Narrative of the Life of Fredrick Douglass, An American Slave*. Boston: American Anti-Slavery Society, 1845.

Durham, Giselle. "Study: Teen Morality Scores Low." ABC News, October 16. Online: http://abcnews.go.com/Health/story?id=117894&page=1#.UaYtDECR8fU.

Editorial Projects in Education Research Center. *Diplomas Count 2008: School to College: Can State P–16 Councils Ease the Transition? Education Week* 27/40, special issue (June 5, 2008). Online: http://www.edweek.org/ew/toc/2008/06/05/index.html.

Education Trust. "The Funding Gap." 2008. Online: http://www.edtrust.org/dc/publication/the-funding-gap-0.

Fears, Darryl. "People of Color Who Never Felt They Were Black." *Washington Post*, December 26, 2002, A01.

Federal Bureau of Investigation, Criminal Justice Information Services Division. "Murder Circumstances by Weapon." Expanded Homicide Data Table 11 in *Crime in the United States, 2011*. Uniform Crime Reports. Clarksburg, WV: FBI CJISD, 2011.

Fisher, Daniel. "Detroit Tops the 2012 List of America's Most Dangerous Cities." *Forbes*, October 18, 2012. Online: http://www.forbes.com/sites/danielfisher/2012/10/18/detroit-tops-the-2012-list-of-americas-most-dangerous-cities/.

Fogel, Robert William. *The Fourth Great Awakening & the Future of Egalitarianism*. Chicago: University of Chicago Press, 2000.

Freeman, Richard B., and Harry J. Holzer. "The Black Youth Employment Crisis: Summary of Findings." In *The Black Youth Employment Crisis*, 3–20. National Bureau of Economic Research project report. Chicago: University of Chicago Press, 1986.

"Frustrated Palestinian Youth Seek New Outlets to Push Change: Israel Conflict and Factional Feud Dim Opportunities." *The Jewish Daily Forward*, May 1, 2013. Online: http://forward.com/articles/175775/frustrated-palestinian-youth-seek-new-outlets-to-p/?p=all#ixzz2UhqGzRhc.

Gates, Henry Louis. "Shared Ancestries Revealed." In "One Family's Roots, a Nation's History," *New York Times*, October 8, 2009. Online: http://roomfordebate.blogs.nytimes.com/2009/10/08/one-familys-roots-a-nations-history/.

Gay, Craig M. *The Way of the Modern World: Why It's Tempting to Live as If God Doesn't Exist*. Grand Rapids: Eerdmans, 1998.

Greene, J. P., and M. Winters. "Public High School Graduation and College Readiness: 1991–2002." Education Working Paper 8. Manhattan Institute for Policy Research, February 2005. Online: http://www.manhattan-institute.org/html/ewp_08.htm.

Gyekye, Kwame. "African Ethics." *The Stanford Encyclopedia of Philosophy*. 2011. Online: http://plato.stanford.edu/entries/african-ethics/.

Bibliography

Henfield, Malik S., Ahmad R. Washington, and Delila Owens. "To Be or Not to Be Gifted." *Gifted Child Today* 32/2 (Spring 2010) 18. Online: http://www.rodneytrice.com/sfbb/articles/gifted.pdf.

Henry, Carl F. H. *Twilight of a Great Civilization*. Westchester, IL: Crossway, 1998.

Holmes, Kristin E. "Norristown Church Members Hit Streets in Antiviolence Effort." Philly.com, July 29, 2011. Online: http://articles.philly.com/2011-07-29/news/29829616_1_ministerium-plans-mentoring-effort.

Hybels, Bill. *Courageous Leadership*. Expanded ed. Grand Rapids: Zondervan, 2009.

Institute for American Values. "Why Marriage Matters, Second Edition: Twenty-Six Conclusions from the Social Sciences." 2005. Online: http://americanvalues.org/pdfs/why_marriage_matters2.pdf.

Jefferson, Thomas. *Notes on the State of Virginia*. 2nd American ed. Philadelphia: printed for Mathew Carey, November 12, 1794.

Johnson, Lyndon B. "To Fulfill These Rights." Commencement address, Howard University, June 4, 1965. Public Papers of the Presidents of the United States, Lyndon B. Johnson, 1965. Vol. 2, entry 301, pp. 635–40. Washington, DC: Government Printing Office, 1966.

Joyce, Kathryn. "Evangelical Rainbow Attack." *The Revealer*, February 17, 2005. Online: http://therevealer.org/archives/1564.

Justin Martyr, and Mark Felix. *We Don't Speak Great Things, We Live Them*. Edited by David Bercot. Amberson, PA: Scroll, 2012.

Kennon, Joshua. "Being an Effective Educator and Communicator Requires an Understanding of the 'Rules' of Your Students' Social and Economic Class According to Ruby Payne's Book *A Framework for Understanding Poverty*." July 24, 2011. Online: http://www.joshuakennon.com/framework-understanding-poverty-ruby-payne/.

———. "New Study Finds the Ability to Delay Gratification Correlates with the Reliability of Adults in a Child's Life." October 20, 2012. Online: http://www.joshuakennon.com/new-study-finds-the-ability-to-delay-gratification-correlates-with-the-reliability-of-adults-in-a-childs-life/.

King, Martin Luther, Jr. "The Purpose of Education." *The Maroon Tiger* (Moorehouse College student paper), January–February, 1947, 10.

———. "Remaining Awake through a Great Revolution." Address at Morehouse College Commencement, Atlanta, June 2, 1959. Online: http://www.brainyquote.com/quotes/quotes/m/martinluth400049.html.

———. *Why We Can't Wait*. New York: Harper, 1964.

Kochhar, Rakesh, Richard Fry, and Paul Taylor. "Wealth Gaps Rise to Record Highs between Whites, Blacks, Hispanics." Pew Research, Social & Demographic Trends, July 26, 2011. Online: http://www.pewsocialtrends.org/2011/07/26/wealth-gaps-rise-to-record-highs-between-whites-blacks-hispanics/.

Larson, David B., and Byron R. Johnson. "Religion: The Forgotten Factor in Cutting Youth Crime and Saving at-Risk Urban Youth." Jeremiah Project

Bibliography

Report 2. Center for Civic Innovation, Manhattan Institute, *1998*. Online: http://www.manhattan-institute.org/html/jpr-98-2.htm.

LeCrae. "Violence." Gravity, September 4, 2012, Reach Records.

Lincoln, Abraham. "'A House Divided': Speech at Springfield, Illinois." In The Collected Works of Abraham Lincoln, edited by Roy P. Basler, 2:461–69. New Brunswick, NJ: Rutgers University Press, 1953.

Madigan, Tim. *The Burning: Massacre, Destruction, and the Tulsa Race Riot of 1921*. New York: St Martin's, 2001.

McDonald, Michael. "2010 General Election Turnout Rates." United States Election Project. Online: http:/elections.gmu.edu/Turnout_2010G.html.

McNulty, Jennifer. "Economists deciphers racial disparities in business ownership." *UC Santa Cruz Currents Online* 10/34 (April 24, 2006). Online: http://currents.ucsc.edu/05-06/04-24/fairlie.asp.

Merton, Thomas. *Gandhi on Non-Violence*. New York: New Directions, 1965.

Miller, A. G. "Black Christianity before the Civil War: Christian History Timeline." *Christianity History & Biography* 62 (April 1, 1999). Online: http://www.ctlibrary.com/ch/1999/issue62/62h026.html.

Morgan, Edmund. *The Puritan Family: Essays on religion and Domestic Relations in Seventeenth-Century New England*. New York: Harper, 1944.

National Healthy Marriage Resource Center. "Testimony of Barbara Dafoe Whitehead, PhD, Co-Director, National Marriage Project Rutgers, the State University of New Jersey before the Committee on Health, Education, Labor and Pensions Subcommittee on Children and Families, U.S. Senate." Online: http://www.healthymarriageinfo.org/resource-detail/index.aspx?rid=3032.

Nielson Company. "The State of the African-American Consumer." Nielson Reports, September 22, 2011. Online: http://www.nielsen.com/us/en/reports/2011/state-of-the-african-american-consumer.html.

Presbyterian Mission Agency. "African-American Members of the Presbyterian Church." Online: http://www.pcusa.org/research/reports/africanamerican.pdf.

Reardon, Sean F. "The Widening Academic Achievement Gap between the Rich and the Poor: New Evidence and Possible Explanations." In *Whither Opportunity?: Rising Inequality, Schools, and Children's Life Chances*, edited by Greg J. Duncan and Richard J. Murnane, 91–116. New York: Russell Sage Foundation, 2011.

Rector, Robert. "Reducing Poverty by Revitalizing Marriage in Low-Income Communities: A Memo to President-Elect Obama." Special Report 45 on Poverty and Inequality and Welfare and Welfare Spending. Heritage Foundation, January 13, 2009. Online: http://www.heritage.org/research/reports/2009/01/reducing-poverty-by-revitalizing-marriage-in-low-income-communities?ac=1.

Roosevelt, Theodore. *Theodore Roosevelt's Letters to His Children*. Edited by Joseph Bucklin. New York: Scribner's, 1919; Bartelby.com, 1998. Online: http://www.bartleby.com/53/.

Bibliography

Sailer, Steve. "Race Now: Part 2: How White Are Blacks? How Black Are Whites." Online: http://www.isteve.com/2002_how_white_are_blacks.htm.

Shapiro, Joseph P., and Andrea R. Wright. "Can Churches Save America?" *U.S. News and World Report*, September 1, 1996. Online: http://www.usnews.com/usnews/culture/articles/960909/archive_034511_3.htm.

Simkin, John. "Freeman's Bureau." Spartacus Educational. Online: http://www.spartacus.schoolnet.co.uk/USASfreemen.htm.

———. "Henry Bibb." Online: http://www.spartacus.schoolnet.co.uk/Sbibb.htm.

———. "John Anderson." Spartacus Educational. Online: http://www.spartacus.schoolnet.co.uk/USASgrandy.htm.

———. "Moses Grandy." Online: http://www.spartacus.schoolnet.co.uk/USASgrandy.htm.

"State of the Black Union 2005: Defining the Agenda, Part 1." Discussion moderated by Tavis Smiley. New Birth Missionary Baptist Church, Lithonia, Georgia, February 26, 2005. Video recording and transcript. Online: http://www.c-spanvideo.org/program/185632-2.

Statistic Brain Research Institute. "Marriage Statistics." Online: http://www.statisticbrain.com/marriage-statistics/.

Toldson, Ivory A., and Kenneth Alonzo Anderson. "The Role of Spirituality, Religion and the African American Church on Educational Outcomes." *The Journal of Negro Education* 79/3 (Summer 2010), 205–13.

Unger, Mike. "Researchers Find Kids Say 'Yes' to Abstinence Only Education." *Penn Current*, December 2, 2010. Online: http://www.upenn.edu/pennnews/current/node/4093.

US Census Bureau. "Census Bureau Reports the Number of Black-Owned Businesses Increased at Triple the National Rate." Press release, February 8, 2011. Online: http://www.census.gov/newsroom/releases/archives/business_ownership/cb11-24.html.

———. "Selected Social Characteristics in the United States: *2007–2011* American Community Survey 5-Year Estimates." American FactFinder. Online: http://factfinder2.census.gov/faces/tableservices/jsf/pages/productview.xhtml?pid=ACS_11_5YR_DP02.

———. "Voting and Registration in the Election of November 2004." Current Population Report, March 2006. Online: http://www.census.gov/prod/2006pubs/p20-556.pdf.

U.S. Department of Education, National Center for Education Statistics. "Trends in First-Time Graduation Rates at Upper Secondary Level, by Country: *1995* and *2000* to *2008*." International Activities Program. Online: https://nces.ed.gov/surveys/international/tables/B_3_02.asp.

———. *The Condition of Education 2004*. NCES 2004–077. Washington, DC: U.S. Government Printing Office, 2004. Online: http://nces.ed.gov/pubsearch/pubsinfo.asp?pubid=2004077.

U.S. Department of Education, Office of Vocational and Adult Education. "High School Reading: Key Issue Brief." 2002.

U.S. Department of Health and Human Services. "Annual Update of the HHS Poverty Guidelines." *Federal Register* 74/14, January 23, 2009, 4199–201.

U.S. Department of Labor, Office of Policy Planning and Research. *The Negro Family: The Case for National Action* ("The Moynihan Report"). Washington, DC: U.S. Government Printing Office, 1965. Online: http://www.dol.gov/dol/aboutdol/history/webid-meynihan.htm.

United States v. Bhagat Singh Thind, 261 U.S. 204 (1923). Online: http://supreme.justia.com/cases/federal/us/261/204/case.html.

Washington, George. *Washington's Farewell Address, in Facsimile, with Transliterations of All the Drafts of Washington, Madison, & Hamilton*. New York Public Library, 1935.

Weems, Lovett H., Jr. "No Shows." *The Christian Century*, September 22, 2010. Online: http://www.christiancentury.org/article/2010-09/no-shows.

West, Cornel. *Race Matters*. Boston: Beacon, 1993.

"Whites Believe They Are Victims of Racism More Often Than Blacks." TuftsNow, May 23, 2011. Online: http://now.tufts.edu/news-releases/whites-believe-they-are-victims-racism-more-o.

Wilcox, W. Bradford. "The Evolution of Divorce." *National Affairs* 1 (Fall 2009). Online: http://www.nationalaffairs.com/publications/detail/the-evolution-of-divorce.

Wilcox, W. Bradford, and Nicholas H. Wolfinger. "Religion and Marriage among African Americans in Urban America." Administration for Children and Families archive, September 27, 2012. http://archive.acf.hhs.gov/healthymarriage/about/aami_wilcox.htm.

Wilkerson, Isabel. *The Warmth of Other Suns: The Epic Story of America's Great Migration*. New York: Random House, 2010.

Wilson, Carl W. *Our Dance Has Turned to Death*. Carol Stream, IL: Tyndale House, 1981.

Wilson, James Q. "Two Nations." Francis Boyer Lecture, presented at the American Enterprise Institute Annual Dinner, December 4, 1997. Online: http://www.aei.org/article/society-and-culture/two-nations-speech/.

Wilson, Jay J., and Ron Wallace. *Black Wallstreet: A Lost Dream*. Tulsa, OK: Black Wallstreet, 1992.

Wintemute, G. J., et al. "The Choice of Weapons in Firearm Suicides." *American Journal of Public Health* 78/7 (1988) 824–26.

www.ingramcontent.com/pod-product-compliance
Lightning Source LLC
Chambersburg PA
CBHW050839160426
43192CB00011B/2084